golf

The Players, The Tournaments, The Records

by
CARLO DE VITO

edited by
SUSAN K. HOM

CIDER MILL
PRESS

BOOK
PUBLISHERS

KENNEBUNKPORT, MAINE

13-Digit ISBN: 978-1-60433-006-9
10-Digit ISBN: 1-60433-006-6

This book may be ordered by mail from the publisher. Please include $2.00 for postage and handling.
Please support your local bookseller first!

Books published by Cider Mill Press Book Publishers are available at special discounts for bulk purchases in the United States by corporations, institutions, and other organizations. For more information, please contact the publisher.

Cider Mill Press Book Publishers
"Where good books are ready for press"
12 Port Farm Road
Kennebunkport, Maine 04046

Visit us on the Web!
www.cidermillpress.com

Design by Jessica Disbrow
All photos courtesy of the Libarary of Congress 2008.
Printed in China

1 2 3 4 5 6 7 8 9 0
First Edition

CONTENTS

INTRODUCTION

On a fine day in the spring, summer, or early autumn, there are few spots more delightful than the terrace in front of our Golf Club. It is a vantage-point peculiarly fitted to the man of philosophic mind: for from it may be seen that varied, never-ending pageant, which men call Golf, in a number of its aspects. To your right, on the first tee, stand the cheery optimists who are about to make their opening drive, happily conscious that even a topped shot will trickle a measurable distance down the steep hill. Away in the valley, directly in front of you, is the lake hole, where these same optimists will be converted to pessimism by the wet splash of a new ball. At your side is the ninth green, with its sinuous undulations which have so often wrecked the returning traveler in sight of home. And at various points within your line of vision are the third tee, the sixth tee, and the sinister bunkers about the eighth green—none of them lacking in food for the reflective mind.

It is on this terrace that the Oldest Member sits, watching the younger generation knocking at the divot.

      ◡   ◡   ◡

Few things
draw two men together
more surely than a

mutual inability
to master golf,

coupled with
an intense and
ever—increasing
love for the game.

—P. G. Wodehouse, from "The Clicking of Cuthbert"

MAJOR TOURNAMENTS

THE MASTERS

◔ In men's golf, the four major tournaments, listed from oldest to youngest, are the Open Championship or the British Open (1860), the U.S. Open (1895), the PGA Championship (1916), and the Masters (1934).

◔ Augusta National Golf Club is the home of the Masters Tournament. The club first opened in December of 1932.

◔ Clifford Roberts liked the name "Masters Tournament" but Bobby Jones preferred "Augusta National Invitation Tournament" because it sounded more humble. Jones's suggestion was used, but the name was too long. It was officially changed in 1939.

◔ On March 22, 1934, the first Masters was played. Horton Smith was the champion. He later won again in 1936.

◔ The final round of the Masters is set for the first Sunday in April.

○ Renowned golfer Bobby Jones teamed up with Alister MacKenzie (architect of Cypress Point in California) to design the course for Augusta National.

○ In 1949, the signature Green Jacket was first awarded to the champion, who was now a member of the elite club. The Green Jackets were worn as early as 1937. If a fan had a question, he could pick out a club member by the bright green color.

○ After the victory, the champion may wear his Green Jacket home, but he must return it the following year. The club will keep his Jacket on hand for his next visit.

○ Holes 11, 12, and 13 were named "Amen Corner" by *Sports Illustrated* writer Herbert Warren Wind in 1958. The phrase "Amen Corner" comes from the jazz record "Shouting at Amen Corner".

○ Wind thought the phrase captured the amazing thrill of Arnold Palmer's performance on the final round. After a controversial ruling made in his favor, Palmer won the Green Jacket that year (the first of four Jackets).

○ If they wish, club members and their families may stay in one of ten cabins located on the Augusta National grounds.

It is an honor to start the ceremonial opening drive of the Masters. Recent starters have included:

Jock Hutchison, 1963–73
Fred McLeod, 1963–76
Gene Sarazen, 1981–99
Byron Nelson, 1981–2001
Ken Venturi, 1983
Sam Snead, 1984–2002
Arnold Palmer, 2007–

In 1997, Tiger Woods, at the age of 21 years, 3 months, 14 days, became the youngest winner of the Masters.

The oldest winner is Jack Nicklaus, at the age of 46 years, 2 months, 23 days, during the 1986 Masters.

Jack Nicklaus has made the most cuts: 37. He also has the most top tens: 22.

Augusta National's
18 Holes

No. 1—Tea Olive

No. 2—Pink Dogwood

No. 3—Flowering Peach

No. 4—Flowering Crab Apple

No. 5—Magnolia

No. 6—Juniper

No. 7—Pampas

No. 8—Yellow Jasmine

No. 9—Carolina Cherry

No. 10—Camellia

No. 11—White Dogwood

No. 12—Golden Bell

No. 13—Azalea

No. 14—Chinese Fir

No. 15—Firethorn

No. 16—Redbud

No. 17—Nandina

No. 18—Holly

Holes-In-One at the Masters

Hole No. 4:
Jeff Sluman, 1992 *(4-iron, 213 yards)*

Hole No. 6:
Leland Gibson, 1954 *(4-iron, 190 yards)*
Billy Joe Patton *(amateur)*, 1954 *(5-iron, 190 yards)*
Charles Coody, 1972 *(5-iron, 190 yards)*
Chris DiMarco, 2004 *(5-iron, 198 yards)*

Hole No. 12:
Claude Harmon, 1947 *(7-iron, 155 yards)*
William Hyndman *(amateur)*, 1959 *(6-iron, 155 yards)*
Curtis Strange, 1988 *(7-iron, 155 yards)*

Hole No. 16:
Ross Somerville *(amateur)*, 1934 *(mashie niblick, 145 yards)*
Willie Goggin, 1935 *(spade mashie, 145 yards)*
Ray Billows *(amateur)*, 1940 *(8-iron, 145 yards)*
John Dawson *(amateur)*, 1949 *(4-iron, 190 yards)*
Clive Clark, 1968 *(2-iron, 190 yards)*
Corey Pavin, 1992 *(8-iron, 140 yards)*
Raymond Floyd, 1996 *(5-iron, 182 yards)*
Padraig Harrington, 2004 *(6-iron, 177 yards)*
Kirk Triplett, 2004 *(6-iron, 177 yards)*
Trevor Immelman, 2005 *(7-iron, 177 yards)*

Double Eagles

Hole No. 8:
Bruce Devlin, 1967, first round *(4-wood, 248 yards)*

Hole No. 13:
Jeff Maggert, 1994, fourth round *(3-iron, 222 yards)*

Hole No. 15:
Gene Sarazen, 1935, fourth round *(4-wood, 235 yards)*

(Sarazen's shot on the 15th hole was famously described as "the shot heard 'round the world".)

Multiple Winners of the Masters

*Sixteen men have the distinction of winning the
Masters more than once through 2007.*

6 wins:

Jack Nicklaus: 1963, 1965, 1966, 1972, 1975, 1986

4 wins:

Arnold Palmer: 1958, 1960, 1962, 1964
Tiger Woods: 1997, 2001, 2002, 2005

3 wins:

Jimmy Demaret: 1940, 1947, 1950
Sam Snead: 1949, 1952, 1954
Gary Player: 1961, 1974, 1978
Nick Faldo: 1989, 1990, 1996

2 wins:

Horton Smith: 1934, 1936
Byron Nelson: 1937, 1942
Ben Hogan: 1951, 1953
Tom Watson: 1977, 1981
Seve Ballesteros: 1980, 1983
Bernhard Langer: 1985, 1993
Ben Crenshaw: 1984, 1995
José María Olazábal: 1994, 1999
Phil Mickelson: 2004, 2006

THE
U.S. OPEN

↖ The United States Golf Association holds the United States Open Championship.

↖ The final round is set for Father's Day, the third Sunday of June.

↖ Host courses feature long, manicured courses, a high cut of rough hills, and pinched fairways.

↖ The first U.S. Open was played on October 4, 1895 at Newport Country Club's nine-hole course.

↖ British golfer Horace Rawlins was the first U.S. Open champion. He was 21 years old.

↖ John J. McDermott was the first native-born American champion. He won the U.S. Open in 1911. He is also the youngest winner of the U.S. Open (19 years, 10 months, 14 days).

✎ The oldest winner is Hale Irwin, at the age of 45 years, 15 days, during the 1990 U.S. Open.

Qualification for the U.S. Open

⟍ Any professional or amateur golfer with an up-to-date USGA Handicap Index that doesn't exceed 1.4 may play in the U.S. Open.

⟍ The field is 156 players. About fifty percent of the field is made up of players who are fully exempt from qualifying.

⟍ There are seventeen full exemption categories, including:
Winners of the U.S. Open for the last ten years
Winners of the other three majors for the last five years
The top 30 from the previous year's PGA Tour money list
The top 15 from the previous year's European Tour money list

⟍ There is no age limit. *(In 2006, Tadd Fujikawa of Hawaii, age 15, was the youngest ever qualifier.)*

⟍ U.S. Open champions automatically qualify for the Masters, the Open Championship (British Open), and the PGA Championship for the next five years.

⟍ The top fifteen finishers at the U.S. Open are automatically qualified for the following year's Open.

⟍ The top eight finishers are automatically qualified for the following season's Masters.

Multiple Winners of the U.S. Open

The following golfers have the distinction of winning the U.S. Open more than once through 2007.

4 wins:

Willie Anderson: 1901, 1903, 1904, 1905

Bobby Jones: 1923, 1926, 1929, 1930

Ben Hogan: 1948, 1950, 1951, 1953

Jack Nicklaus: 1962, 1967, 1972, 1980

3 wins:

Hale Irwin: 1974, 1979, 1990

2 wins:

Alex Smith: 1906, 1910

John J. McDermott: 1911, 1912

Walter Hagen: 1914, 1919

Gene Sarazen: 1922, 1932

Ralph Guldahl: 1937, 1938

Cary Middlecoff: 1949, 1956

Julius Boros: 1952, 1963

Billy Casper: 1959, 1966

Lee Trevino: 1968, 1971

Andy North: 1978, 1985

Curtis Strange: 1988, 1989

Ernie Els: 1994, 1997

Lee Janzen: 1993, 1998

Payne Stewart: 1991, 1999

Tiger Woods: 2000, 2002

Retief Goosen: 2001, 2004

Host Clubs of the U.S. Open

2014
Pinehurst Resort,
Course No. 2
*(Village of Pinehurst,
North Carolina)*

2013
Merion Golf Club,
East Course
(Ardmore, Pennsylvania)

2012
The Olympic Club,
Lake Course
(San Francisco, California)

2011
Congressional Country Club,
Blue Course
(Bethesda, Maryland)

2010
Pebble Beach Golf Links
(Pebble Beach, California)

2009
Bethpage State Park,
Black Course
(Farmingdale, New York)

2008
Torrey Pines Golf Course,
South Course
(La Jolla, California)

2007
Oakmont Country Club
(Oakmont, Pennsylvania)

2006
Winged Foot Golf Club,
West Course
(Mamaroneck, New York)

2005
Pinehurst Resort,
Course No. 2
*(Village of Pinehurst, North
Carolina)*

2004
Shinnecock Hills Golf Club
(Southampton, New York)

2003
Olympia Fields Country Club,
North Course
(Olympia Fields, Illinois)

2002
Bethpage State Park,
Black Course
(Farmingdale, New York)

2001
Southern Hills Country Club
(Tulsa, Oklahoma)

2000
Pebble Beach Golf Links
(Pebble Beach, California)

1999
Pinehurst Resort,
Course No. 2
*(Village of Pinehurst,
North Carolina)*

1998
The Olympic Club,
Lake Course
(San Francisco, California)

1997
Congressional Country Club,
Blue Course
(Bethesda, Maryland)

1996
Oakland Hills Country Club,
South Course
(Bloomfield Hills, Michigan)

1995
Shinnecock Hills Golf Club
(Southampton, New York)

1994
Oakmont Country Club
(Oakmont, Pennsylvania)

1993
Baltusrol Golf Club,
Lower Course
(Springfield, New Jersey)

1992
Pebble Beach Golf Links
(Pebble Beach, California)

1991
Hazeltine National Golf Club
(Chaska, Minnesota)

1990
Medinah Country Club,
Course No. 3
(Medinah, Illinois)

1989
Oak Hill Country Club,
East Course
(Rochester, New York)

1988
The Country Club,
Course No. 2
(Brookline, Massachusetts)

1987
The Olympic Club
(San Francisco, California)

1986
Shinnecock Hills Golf Club
(Southampton, New York)

1985
Oakland Hills Country Club,
South Course
(Bloomfield Hills, Michigan)

1984
Winged Foot Golf Club,
West Course
(Mamaroneck, New York)

1983
Oakmont Country Club
(Oakmont, Pennsylvania)

1982
Pebble Beach Golf Links
(Pebble Beach, California)

1981
Merion Golf Club,
East Course
(Ardmore, Pennsylvania)

1980
Baltusrol Golf Club,
Lower Course
(Springfield, New Jersey)

1979
Inverness Club
(Toledo, Ohio)

1978
Cherry Hills Country Club
(Englewood, Colorado)

1977
Southern Hills Country Club
(Tulsa, Oklahoma)

1976
Atlanta Athletic Club,
Highlands Course
(Duluth, Georgia)

1975
Medinah Country Club,
Course No. 3
(Medinah, Illinois)

1974
Winged Foot Golf Club,
West Course
(Mamaroneck, New York)

1973
Oakmont Country Club
(Oakmont, Pennsylvania)

1972
Pebble Beach Golf Links
(Pebble Beach, California)

1971
Merion Golf Club,
East Course
(Ardmore, Pennsylvania)

1970
Hazeltine National Golf Club
(Chaska, Minnesota)

1969
Champions Golf Club,
Cypress Creek Course
(Houston, Texas)

1968
Oak Hill Country Club,
East Course
(Rochester, New York)

1967
Baltusrol Golf Club,
Lower Course
(Springfield, New Jersey)

1966
The Olympic Club,
Lake Course
(San Francisco, California)

1965
Bellerive Country Club
(St. Louis, Missouri)

1964
Congressional Country Club,
Blue Course
(Bethesda, Maryland)

1963
The Country Club,
Course No. 2
(Brookline, Massachusetts)

1962
Oakmont Country Club
(Oakmont, Pennsylvania)

1961
Oakland Hills Country Club,
South Course
(Bloomfield Hills, Michigan)

1960
Cherry Hills Country Club
(Englewood, Colorado)

1959
Winged Foot Golf Club,
West Course
(Mamaroneck, New York)

1958
Southern Hills Country Club
(Tulsa, Oklahoma)

1957
Inverness Club
(Toledo, Ohio)

1956
Oak Hill Country Club,
East Course
(Rochester, New York)

1955
The Olympic Club,
Lake Course
(San Francisco, California)

1954
Baltusrol Golf Club,
Lower Course
(Springfield, New Jersey)

1953
Oakmont Country Club
(Oakmont, Pennsylvania)

1952
Northwood Club
(Dallas, Texas)

1951
Oakland Hills Country Club,
South Course
(Bloomfield Hills, Michigan)

1950
Merion Golf Club,
East Course
(Ardmore, Pennsylvania)

1949
Medinah Country Club,
Course No. 3
(Medinah, Illinois)

1948
Riviera Country Club
(Pacific Palisades, California)

1947
St. Louis Country Club
(St. Louis, Missouri)

1946
Canterbury Golf Club
(Cleveland, Ohio)

1942—45
Not played due to World War II

1941
Colonial Country Club
(Fort Worth, Texas)

1940
Canterbury Golf Club
(Cleveland, Ohio)

1939
Philadelphia Country Club,
Spring Mill Course
(Gladwyne, Pennsylvania)

1938
Cherry Hills Country Club
(Englewood, Colorado)

1937
Oakland Hills Country Club,
South Course
(Bloomfield Hills, Michigan)

1936
Baltusrol Golf Club,
Upper Course
(Springfield, New Jersey)

1935
Oakmont Country Club
(Oakmont, Pennsylvania)

1934
Merion Golf Club,
East Course
(Ardmore, Pennsylvania)

1933
North Shore Country Club
(Glenview, Illinois)

1932
Fresh Meadow Country Club
(Flushing, New York)

1931
Inverness Club
(Toledo, Ohio)

1930
Interlachen Country Club
(Edina, Minnesota)

1929
Winged Foot Golf Club,
West Course
(Mamaroneck, New York)

1928
Olympia Fields Country Club,
North Course
(Olympia Fields, Illinois)

1927
Oakmont Country Club
(Oakmont, Pennsylvania)

1926
Scioto Country Club
(Columbus, Ohio)

1925
Worcester Country Club
(Worcester, Massachusetts)

1924
Oakland Hills Country Club,
South Course
(Bloomfield Hills, Michigan)

1923
Inwood Country Club
(Inwood, New York)

1922
Skokie Country Club
(Glencoe, Illinois)

1921
Columbia Country Club
(Chevy Chase, Maryland)

1920
Inverness Club
(Toledo, Ohio)

1919
Brae Burn Country Club,
Main Course
(West Newton, Massachusetts)

1917—18
Not played due to World War I

1916
Minikahda Club
(Minneapolis, Minnesota)

1915
Baltusrol Golf Club
(Springfield, New Jersey)

1914
Midlothian Country Club
(Midlothian, Illinois)

1913
The Country Club,
Course No. 2
(Brookline, Massachusetts)

1912
The Country Club of Buffalo
(Buffalo, New York)

1911
Chicago Golf Club
(Wheaton, Illinois)

1910
Philadelphia Cricket Club,
St. Martin's Course
(Philadelphia, Pennsylvania)

1909
Englewood Golf Club
(Englewood, New Jersey)

1908
Myopia Hunt Club
(South Hamilton, Massachusetts)

1907
Philadelphia Cricket Club,
St. Martin's Course
(Philadelphia, Pennsylvania)

1906
Onwentsia Club
(Lake Forest, Illinois)

1905
Myopia Hunt Club
(South Hamilton, Massachusetts)

1904
Glen View Club
(Golf, Illinois)

1903
Baltusrol Golf Club
(Springfield, New Jersey)

1902
Garden City Golf Club
(Garden City, New York)

1901
Myopia Hunt Club
(South Hamilton, Massachusetts)

1900
Chicago Golf Club
(Wheaton, Illinois)

1899
Baltimore Country Club,
Roland Park Course
(Baltimore, Maryland)

1898
Myopia Hunt Club
(South Hamilton, Massachusetts)

1897
Chicago Golf Club
(Wheaton, Illinois)

1896
Shinnecock Hills Golf Club
(Southampton, New York)

1895
Newport Country Club
(Newport, Rhode Island)

THE OPEN CHAMPIONSHIP

◡ The Open Championship is the official name of this major tournament. Outside the United Kingdom, it's called the British Open.

◡ In men's golf, the Open Championship is the oldest of the four major tournaments.

◡ It is the only major held outside the United States. The R&A organizes the Open Championship. The R&A is the governing body of golf outside the United States and Mexico.

◡ The Open is held annually on one of nine links courses in the United Kingdom.

◡ It is always scheduled for the weekend of the third Friday in July. The Open is the third major to take place each year following the Masters and the U.S. Open. It is held before the PGA Championship.

◯ Golfers tied at the end of regulation must compete in a four-hole play-off.

◯ On October 17, 1860, the first Open was held at Prestwick Golf Club. The tournament lasted a single day.

◯ Only professionals were allowed to participate. There was a field of eight. The golfers played three rounds on the twelve-hole course. The Open was 32 holes until 1892 when it was increased to 72 holes.

◯ Willie Park Senior defeated Old Tom Morris by two strokes at the first Open.

◯ The prize has evolved over the years from the Champion's Belt (a red leather belt with a silver buckle) to The Golf Champion Trophy or The Claret Jug.

The Field

The Open has a field of 156.

. . . . .

About two thirds of the field consists of leading golfers who are given exemptions.

. . . . .

"Local Qualifying" and "International Qualifying" players make up the final third of the field.

The Rota

Course locations are selected according to the ending years.

(0, 5)—Old Course at St. Andrews, Scotland
(1, 6)—England
(2, 7)—Scotland
(3, 8)—England
(4, 9)—Scotland

Courses in the Rota

Old Course at St. Andrews:

Considered by many to be the "Home of Golf," golfers have been playing here since the 15th century. There are vast greens and plenty of bunkers, including the Hell Bunker on the 14th hole, the largest one on the Old Course.

Carnoustie Golf Links, Championship Course:

This Scottish course first held the Open in 1931. It also hosted the 2007 Open. Carnoustie's course is challenging with long holes, numerous bunkers, and two burns (streams).

Muirfield:

In 1891, The Honourable Company of Edinburgh Golfers settled into their third home. The course was designed by Harry Colt. The front nine holes run clockwise on the outer loop while the back nine holes run counterclockwise. The wind and deep bunkers present a continual challenge to the golfer.

The Westin Turnberry Resort, Ailsa Course:

This famous course is situated on the southwest coast of Scotland. An old lighthouse lies beyond the 9th hole. The 10th hole is famous for its "fried egg"-shaped bunker.

Royal Troon Golf Club, Old Course:

In the Scottish tradition, Royal Troon's layout has nine holes out along the coast and nine holes back on the return inland. Gene Sarazen made a hole-in-one at the 8th hole in the 1973 Open. It is described as the "Postage Stamp" hole because of the tiny green.

Royal St. George's Golf Club:

Located in the town of Sandwich in the county of Kent, this course offers uneven lies, pot bunkers, a short hole on the 6th (nicknamed the Maiden), and a stream near the 14th hole (nicknamed the Suez).

Royal Birkdale Golf Club:

This course in northwest England boasts beautiful fairways lined with dunes and a 5th hole surrounded by a semicircle of bunkers. It will host the 2008 Open.

Royal Lytham & St. Annes Golf Club:

Royal Lytham's course is in Lancashire. The course starts with a par 3 on the first hole. There are over 100 deep bunkers at Royal Lytham. It is definitely a challenging course.

Royal Liverpool Golf Club:

Hoylake has a closing stretch with two par 5s and three par 4s, an internal out of bounds area, and rough terrain at the far end of the links.

Former Courses in the Rota

Prestwick Golf Club:

Although it was the founding club in the Open, it was dropped from the rota in 1925. Prestwick hosted 24 championships.

Musselburgh Links:

This public course was the second home of The Honourable Company of Edinburgh Golfers. It dropped out of the rota after Muirfield was constructed.

Royal Cinque Ports Golf Club:

This historic course is located in the town of Deal in Kent, England.

Prince's Golf Club:

It is located in Sandwich, Kent in England. The 1932 Open was the only Open held here.

Royal Portrush Golf Club:

Harry Colt designed the Dunluce links at Royal Portrush in Northern Ireland. Its only Open was in 1951.

Host Courses of the Open Championship

2010
St. Andrews
(St. Andrews, Fife, Scotland)

2009
The Westin Turnberry Resort
(Ayrshire, Scotland)

2008
Royal Birkdale Golf Club
(Southport, England)

2007
Carnoustie Golf Links
(Carnoustie, Scotland)

2006
Royal Liverpool Golf Club
*(Hoylake Wirral,
Merseyside, England)*

2005
St. Andrews
(St. Andrews, Fife, Scotland)

2004
Royal Troon Golf Club
(Ayrshire, Scotland)

2003
Royal St. George's Golf Club
(Sandwich, Kent, England)

2002
Muirfield
(Gullane, East Lothian, Scotland)

2001
Royal Lytham
& St. Annes Golf Club
*(Lytham, St. Annes,
Lancashire, England)*

2000
St. Andrews
(St. Andrews, Fife, Scotland)

1999
Carnoustie Golf Links
(Carnoustie, Scotland)

1998
Royal Birkdale Golf Club
(Southport, England)

1997
Royal Troon Golf Club
(Ayrshire, Scotland)

1996
Royal Lytham
& St. Annes Golf Club
(Lytham, St. Annes,
Lancashire, England)

1995
St. Andrews
(St. Andrews, Fife, Scotland)

1994
The Westin Turnberry Resort
(Ayrshire, Scotland)

1993
Royal St. George's Golf Club
(Sandwich, Kent, England)

1992
Muirfield
(Gullane, East Lothian, Scotland)

1991
Royal Birkdale Golf Club
(Southport, England)

1990
St. Andrews
(St. Andrews, Fife, Scotland)

1989
Royal Troon Golf Club
(Ayrshire, Scotland)

1988
Royal Lytham
& St. Annes Golf Club
(Lytham, St. Annes,
Lancashire, England)

1987
Muirfield
(Gullane, East Lothian, Scotland)

1986
The Westin Turnberry Resort
(Ayrshire, Scotland)

1985
Royal St. George's Golf Club
(Sandwich, Kent, England)

1984
St. Andrews
(St. Andrews, Fife, Scotland)

1983
Royal Birkdale Golf Club
(Southport, England)

1982
Royal Troon Golf Club
(Ayrshire, Scotland)

1981
Royal St. George's Golf Club
(Sandwich, Kent, England)

1980
Muirfield
(Gullane, East Lothian, Scotland)

1979
Royal Lytham
& St. Annes Golf Club
*(Lytham, St. Annes,
Lancashire, England)*

1978
St. Andrews
(St. Andrews, Fife, Scotland)

1977
The Westin Turnberry Resort
(Ayrshire, Scotland)

1976
Royal Birkdale Golf Club
(Southport, England)

1975
Carnoustie Golf Links
(Carnoustie, Scotland)

1974
Royal Lytham
& St. Annes Golf Club
(Lytham, St. Annes,
Lancashire, England)

1973
Royal Troon Golf Club
(Ayrshire, Scotland)

1972
Muirfield
(Gullane, East Lothian, Scotland)

1971
Royal Birkdale Golf Club
(Southport, England)

1970
St. Andrews
(St. Andrews, Fife, Scotland)

1969
Royal Lytham
& St. Annes Golf Club
(Lytham, St. Annes,
Lancashire, England)

1968
Carnoustie Golf Links
(Carnoustie, Scotland)

1967
Royal Liverpool Golf Club
(Hoylake Wirral,
Merseyside, England)

1966
Muirfield
(Gullane, East Lothian, Scotland)

1965
Royal Birkdale Golf Club
(Southport, England)

1964
St. Andrews
(St. Andrews, Fife, Scotland)

1963
Royal Lytham
& St. Annes Golf Club
(Lytham, St. Annes,
Lancashire, England)

1962
Royal Troon Golf Club
(Ayrshire, Scotland)

1961
Royal Birkdale Golf Club
(Southport, England)

1960
St. Andrews
(St. Andrews, Fife, Scotland)

1959
Muirfield
(Gullane, East Lothian, Scotland)

1958
Royal Lytham
& St. Annes Golf Club
*(Lytham, St. Annes,
Lancashire, England)*

1957
St. Andrews
(St. Andrews, Fife, Scotland)

1956
Royal Liverpool Golf Club
*(Hoylake Wirral,
Merseyside, England)*

1955
St. Andrews
(St. Andrews, Fife, Scotland)

1954
Royal Birkdale Golf Club
(Southport, England)

1953
Carnoustie Golf Links
(Carnoustie, Scotland)

1952
Royal Lytham
& St. Annes Golf Club
*(Lytham, St. Annes,
Lancashire, England)*

1951
Royal Portrush Golf Club
(Antrim, Northern Ireland)

1950
Royal Troon Golf Club
(Ayrshire, Scotland)

1949
Royal St. George's Golf Club
(Sandwich, Kent, England)

1948
Muirfield
(Gullane, East Lothian, Scotland)

1947
Royal Liverpool Golf Club
*(Hoylake Wirral,
Merseyside, England)*

1946
St. Andrews
(St. Andrews, Fife, Scotland)

1940—1945
Not played due to World War II

1939
St. Andrews
(St. Andrews, Fife, Scotland)

1938
Royal St. George's Golf Club
(Sandwich, Kent, England)

1937
Carnoustie Golf Links
Carnoustie, Scotland)

1936
Royal Liverpool Golf Club
*(Hoylake Wirral,
Merseyside, England)*

1935
Muirfield
(Gullane, East Lothian, Scotland)

1934
Royal St. George's Golf Club
(Sandwich, Kent, England)

1933
St. Andrews
(St. Andrews, Fife, Scotland)

1932
Prince's Golf Club
(Sandwich, Kent, England)

1931
Carnoustie Golf Links
(Carnoustie, Scotland)

1930
Royal Liverpool Golf Club
*(Hoylake Wirral,
Merseyside, England)*

1929
Muirfield
(Gullane, East Lothian, Scotland)

1928 Royal St. George's
Golf Club
(Sandwich, Kent, England)

1927
St. Andrews
(St. Andrews, Fife, Scotland)

1926
Royal Lytham
& St. Annes Golf Club
*(Lytham, St. Annes,
Lancashire, England)*

1925
Prestwick Golf Club
(Ayrshire, Scotland)

1924
Royal Liverpool Golf Club
*(Hoylake Wirral,
Merseyside, England)*

1923
Royal Troon Golf Club
(Ayrshire, Scotland)

1922
Royal St. George's Golf Club
(Sandwich, Kent, England)

1921
St. Andrews
(St. Andrews, Fife, Scotland)

1920
Royal Cinque Ports Golf Club
(Deal, Kent, England)

1915—1919
Not played due to World War I

1914
Prestwick Golf Club
(Ayrshire, Scotland)

1913
Royal Liverpool Golf Club
*(Hoylake Wirral,
Merseyside, England)*

1912
Muirfield
(Gullane, East Lothian, Scotland)

1911
Royal St. George's Golf Club
(Sandwich, Kent, England)

1910
St. Andrews
(St. Andrews, Fife, Scotland)

1909
Royal Cinque Ports Golf Club
(Deal, Kent, England)

1908
Prestwick Golf Club
(Ayrshire, Scotland)

1907
Royal Liverpool Golf Club
*(Hoylake Wirral,
Merseyside, England)*

1906
Muirfield
(Gullane, East Lothian, Scotland)

1905
St. Andrews
(St. Andrews, Fife, Scotland)

1904
Royal St. George's Golf Club
(Sandwich, Kent, England)

1903
Prestwick Golf Club
(Ayrshire, Scotland)

1902
Royal Liverpool Golf Club
*(Hoylake Wirral,
Merseyside, England)*

1901
Muirfield
(Gullane, East Lothian, Scotland)

1900
St. Andrews
(St. Andrews, Fife, Scotland)

1899
Royal St. George's Golf Club
(Sandwich, Kent, England)

1898
Prestwick Golf Club
(Ayrshire, Scotland)

1897
Royal Liverpool Golf Club
(Hoylake Wirral,
Merseyside, England)

1896
Muirfield
(Gullane, East Lothian, Scotland)

1895
St. Andrews
(St. Andrews, Fife, Scotland)

1894
Royal St. George's Golf Club
(Sandwich, Kent, England)

1893
Prestwick Golf Club
(Ayrshire, Scotland)

1892
Muirfield
(Gullane, East Lothian, Scotland)

1891
St. Andrews
(St. Andrews, Fife, Scotland)

1890
Prestwick Golf Club
(Ayrshire, Scotland)

1889
Musselburgh Links
(East Lothian, Scotland)

1888
St. Andrews
(St. Andrews, Fife, Scotland)

1887
Prestwick Golf Club
(Ayrshire, Scotland)

1886
Musselburgh Links
(East Lothian, Scotland)

1885
St. Andrews
(St. Andrews, Fife, Scotland)

1884
Prestwick Golf Club
(Ayrshire, Scotland)

1883
Musselburgh Links
(East Lothian, Scotland)

1882
St. Andrews
(St. Andrews, Fife, Scotland)

1881
Prestwick Golf Club
(Ayrshire, Scotland)

1880
Musselburgh Links
(East Lothian, Scotland)

1879
St. Andrews
(St. Andrews, Fife, Scotland)

1878
Prestwick Golf Club
(Ayrshire, Scotland)

1877
Musselburgh Links
(East Lothian, Scotland)

1876
St. Andrews
(St. Andrews, Fife, Scotland)

1875
Prestwick Golf Club
(Ayrshire, Scotland)

1874
Musselburgh Links
(East Lothian, Scotland)

1873
St. Andrews
(St. Andrews, Fife, Scotland)

1872
Prestwick Golf Club
(Ayrshire, Scotland)

1871
No Championship

1870
Prestwick Golf Club
(Ayrshire, Scotland)

1869
Prestwick Golf Club
(Ayrshire, Scotland)

1868
Prestwick Golf Club
(Ayrshire, Scotland)

1867
Prestwick Golf Club
(Ayrshire, Scotland)

1866
Prestwick Golf Club
(Ayrshire, Scotland)

1865
Prestwick Golf Club
(Ayrshire, Scotland)

1864
Prestwick Golf Club
(Ayrshire, Scotland)

1863
Prestwick Golf Club
(Ayrshire, Scotland)

1862
Prestwick Golf Club
(Ayrshire, Scotland)

1861
Prestwick Golf Club
(Ayrshire, Scotland)

1860
Prestwick Golf Club
(Ayrshire, Scotland)

THE PGA CHAMPIONSHIP

↘ The PGA Championship is set for the fourth weekend after the British Open. It is typically held in late August.

↘ PGA Champions are automatically qualified for the other three majors for the next five years, as well as any future PGA Championships for the rest of their life.

↘ Siwanoy Country Club in Bronxville, New York hosted the first PGA Championship in 1916. Jim Barnes was the first PGA Champion.

↘ The PGA Championship evolved from a match play event to a stroke play event (first played in 1958).

↘ The best 72-hole score record, 265, is held by David Toms in the 2001 PGA Championship.

⤙ The best 72-hole score in relation to par record, 18 under (270) by Tiger Woods in the 2000 and 2006 PGA Championships.

⤙ John Mahaffey has the record for the largest comeback by a winner (7 shots). He won in the 1978 PGA Championship.

⤙ Both Jack Nicklaus and Raymond Floyd made 7 cuts, the record for the most cuts made in a PGA Championship.

⤙ The record for largest margin of victory is held by Jack Nicklaus with 7 shots in the 1980 PGA Championship.

Multiple Winners of the PGA Championship

The following men have won the PGA Championship more than once through 2007.

5 wins:

Walter Hagen: 1921, 1924, 1925, 1926, 1927

Jack Nicklaus: 1963, 1971, 1973, 1975, 1980

4 wins:

Tiger Woods: 1999, 2000, 2006, 2007

3 wins:

Gene Sarazen: 1922, 1923, 1933

Sam Snead: 1942, 1949, 1951

2 wins:

Jim Barnes: 1916, 1919

Leo Diegel: 1928, 1929

Raymond Floyd: 1969, 1982

Ben Hogan: 1946, 1948

Byron Nelson: 1940, 1945

Larry Nelson: 1981, 1987

Gary Player:1962, 1972

Nick Price: 1992, 1994

Paul Runyan: 1934, 1938

Denny Shute: 1936, 1937

Vijay Singh: 1998, 2004

Dave Stockton: 1970, 1976

Lee Trevino: 1974, 1984

Host Clubs of the PGA Championship

2011
Atlanta Athletic Club
(Duluth, Georgia)

2010
Whistling Straits Country Club
(Kohler, Wisconsin)

2009
Hazeltine National Golf Club
(Chaska, Minnesota)

2008
Oakland Hills Country Club
(Bloomfield Hills, Michigan)

2007
Southern Hills Country Club
(Tulsa, Oklahoma)

2006
Medinah Country Club
(Medinah, Illinois)

2005
Baltusrol Golf Club
(Springfield, New Jersey)

2004
Whistling Straits Country Club
(Kohler, Wisconsin)

2003
Oak Hill Country Club
(Rochester, New York)

2002
Hazeltine National Golf Club
(Chaska, Minnesota)

2001
Atlanta Athletic Club
(Duluth, Georgia)

2000
Valhalla Golf Club
(Louisville, Kentucky)

1999
Medinah Country Club
(Medinah, Illinois)

1998
Sahalee Country Club
(Redmond, Washington)

1997
Winged Foot Golf Club
(Mamaroneck, New York)

1996
Valhalla Golf Club
(Louisville, Kentucky)

1995
Riviera Country Club
(Pacific Palisades, California)

1994
Southern Hills Country Club
(Tulsa, Oklahoma)

1993
Inverness Club
(Toledo, Ohio)

1992
Bellerive Country Club
(St. Louis, Missouri)

1991
Crooked Stick Golf Club
(Carmel, Indiana)

1990
Shoal Creek Golf
and Country Club
(Birmingham, Alabama)

1989
Kemper Lakes Golf Club
(Hawthorn Woods, Illinois)

1988
Oak Tree Golf Club
(Edmond, Oklahoma)

1987
PGA National Resort and Spa
(Palm Beach Gardens, Florida)

1986
Inverness Club
(Toledo, Ohio)

1985
Cherry Hills Country Club
(Englewood, Colorado)

1984
Shoal Creek Golf
and Country Club
(Birmingham, Alabama)

1983
Riviera Country Club
(Pacific Palisades, California)

1982
Southern Hills Country Club
(Tulsa, Oklahoma)

1981
Atlanta Athletic Club
(Duluth, Georgia)

1980
Oak Hill Country Club
(Rochester, New York)

1979
Oakland Hills Country Club,
South Course
(Bloomfield Hills, Michigan)

1978
Oakmont Country Club
(Oakmont, Pennsylvania)

1977
Pebble Beach Golf Links
(Pebble Beach, California)

1976
Congressional Country Club
(Bethesda, Maryland)

1975
Firestone Country Club
(Akron, Ohio)

1974
Tanglewood Park
(Winston-Salem, North Carolina)

1973
Canterbury Golf Club
(Cleveland, Ohio)

1972
Oakland Hills Country Club
(Bloomfield Hills, Michigan)

1971
PGA National Resort and Spa
(Palm Beach Gardens, Florida)

1970
Southern Hills Country Club
(Tulsa, Oklahoma)

1969
NCR Country Club
(Dayton, Ohio)

1968
Pecan Valley Golf Club
(San Antonio, Texas)

1967
Columbine Country Club
(Littleton, Colorado)

1966
Firestone Country Club
(Akron, Ohio)

1965
Laurel Valley Golf Club
(Ligonier, Pennsylvania)

1964
Columbus Country Club
(Columbus, Ohio)

1963
Dallas Athletic Club
(Mesquite, Texas)

1962
Aronimink Golf Club
(Newtown Square, Pennsylvania)

1961
Olympia Fields Country Club
(Olympia Fields, Illinois)

1960
Firestone Country Club
(Akron, Ohio)

1959
Minneapolis Golf Club
(St. Louis Park, Minnesota)

1958
Llanerch Country Club
(Havertown, Pennsylvania)

1957
Miami Valley Golf Club
(Dayton, Ohio)

1956
Blue Hill Country Club
(Canton, Massachusetts)

1955
Meadowbrook Country Club
(Detroit, Michigan)

1954
Keller Golf Club
(St. Paul, Minnesota)

1953
Birmingham Country Club
(Birmingham, Michigan)

1952
Big Spring Country Club
(Louisville, Kentucky)

1951
Oakmont Country Club
(Oakmont, Pennsylvania)

1950
Scioto Country Club
(Columbus, Ohio)

1949
Hermitage Country Club
(Richmond, Virginia)

1948
Norwood Hills Country Club
(St. Louis, Missouri)

1947
Plum Hollow Country Club
(Southfield, Michigan)

1946
Portland Golf Club
(Portland, Oregon)

1945
Moraine Country Club
(Dayton, Ohio)

1944
Manito Golf and Country Club
(Spokane, Washington)

1943
Not played

1942
Seaview Country Club
(Atlantic City, New Jersey)

1941
Cherry Hills Country Club
(Englewood, Colorado)

1940
Hershey Country Club
(Hershey, Pennsylvania)

1939
Pomonok Country Club
(Flushing, New York)

1938
Shawnee Country Club
*(Shawnee-on-Delaware,
Pennsylvania)*

1937
Pittsburgh Field Club
(Aspinwall, Pennsylvania)

1936
Pinehurst Resort
*(Village of Pinehurst,
North Carolina)*

1935
Twin Hills Golf
and Country Club
(Oklahoma City, Oklahoma)

1934
Park Country Club
(Williamsville, New York)

1933
Blue Mound Golf
and Country Club
(Wauwatosa, Wisconsin)

1932
Keller Golf Club
(St. Paul, Minnesota)

1931
Wannamoisett Country Club
(Rumford, Rhode Island)

1930
Fresh Meadow Country Club
(Flushing, New York)

1929
Hillcrest Country Club
(Los Angeles, California)

1928
Five Farms Country Club
(Baltimore, Maryland)

1927
Cedar Crest Country Club,
now called Cedar Crest Park
(Dallas, Texas)

1926
Salisbury Golf Club
(Westbury, New York)

1925
Olympia Fields Country Club
(Olympia Fields, Illinois)

1924
French Lick Country Club,
now called French Lick
Springs Resort
(French Lick, Indiana)

1923
Pelham Country Club
(Pelham Manor, New York)

1922
Oakmont Country Club
(Oakmont, Pennsylvania)

1921
Inwood Country Club
(Inwood, New York)

1920
Flossmoor Country Club
(Flossmoor, Illinois)

1919
Engineers Country Club
(Roslyn Harbor, New York)

1917—18
Not played

1916
Siwanoy Country Club
(Bronxville, New York)

Qualification for the PGA Championship

- All former PGA Champions.

- Winners of the last five U.S. Opens.

- Winners of the last five Masters.

- Winners of the last five Open Championships.

- The last Senior PGA Champion.

- The low 15 scorers and ties in the previous PGA Championship.

● The 20 low scorers in the last PGA Professional National Championship.

● The 70 leaders in official money standings. (This period starts one week prior to the previous year's PGA Championship and finishes two weeks prior to the current year's PGA Championship.)

● Members of the most recent United States Ryder Cup team.

● Winners of tournaments co-sponsored or approved by the PGA Tour since the previous PGA Championship (not including pro-am and team competitions).

● The PGA of America may invite additional players not included in the categories listed above.

● The total field is 156 players.

● There is a list of alternates comprised of players who are ranked below the 70th place in official money standings.

THE
CANADIAN
OPEN

✎ The Canadian Open was first held in 1904.

✎ It is usually set for mid-September.

✎ The prize evolved from the Canadian Amateur Trophy (1895 to 1907) to the Earl Grey Trophy (first awarded in 1908). Today it is called the Bell Canadian Open Trophy (first awarded in 1994).

✎ Arnold Palmer had a Canadian Open victory in 1955.

✎ Lee Trevino won the tournament three times (1971, 1977, 1979).

✎ Greg Norman won the Canadian Open in 1984 and 1992.

✎ In 2000, Tiger Woods won the Bell Canadian Open with a score of 266. (It was called the Bell Canadian Open during 1994 to 2005, after the sponsor Bell Canada.)

Host Clubs of the Canadian Open

2007
Angus Glen Golf Club,
North Course
(Markham, Ontario)

2006
Hamilton Golf a
nd Country Club
(Ancaster, Ontario)

2005
Shaughnessy Golf
and Country Club
(Vancouver, British Columbia)

2004
Glen Abbey Golf Club
(Oakville, Ontario)

2003
Hamilton Golf
and Country Club
(Ancaster, Ontario)

2002
Angus Glen Golf Club,
South Course
(Markham, Ontario)

2001
Royal Montreal Golf Club
(Ile Bizard, Quebec)

2000
Glen Abbey Golf Club
(Oakville, Ontario)

1999
Glen Abbey Golf Club
(Oakville, Ontario)

1998
Glen Abbey Golf Club
(Oakville, Ontario)

1997
Royal Montreal Golf Club
(Ile Bizard, Quebec)

1996
Glen Abbey Golf Club
(Oakville, Ontario)

1995
Glen Abbey Golf Club
(Oakville, Ontario)

1994
Glen Abbey Golf Club
(Oakville, Ontario)

1993
Glen Abbey Golf Club
(Oakville, Ontario)

1992
Glen Abbey Golf Club
(Oakville, Ontario)

1991
Glen Abbey Golf Club
(Oakville, Ontario)

1990
Glen Abbey Golf Club
(Oakville, Ontario)

1989
Glen Abbey Golf Club
(Oakville, Ontario)

1988
Glen Abbey Golf Club
(Oakville, Ontario)

1987
Glen Abbey Golf Club
(Oakville, Ontario)

1986
Glen Abbey Golf Club
(Oakville, Ontario)

1985
Glen Abbey Golf Club
(Oakville, Ontario)

1984
Glen Abbey Golf Club
(Oakville, Ontario)

1983
Glen Abbey Golf Club
(Oakville, Ontario)

1982
Glen Abbey Golf Club
(Oakville, Ontario)

1981
Glen Abbey Golf Club
(Oakville, Ontario)

1980
Royal Montreal Golf Club
(Ile Bizard, Quebec)

1979
Glen Abbey Golf Club
(Oakville, Ontario)

1978
Glen Abbey Golf Club
(Oakville, Ontario)

1977
Glen Abbey Golf Club
(Oakville, Ontario)

1976
Essex Golf and Country Club
(LaSalle, Ontario)

1975
Royal Montreal Golf Club
(Ile Bizard, Quebec)

1974
Mississaugua Golf
and Country Club
(Mississauga, Ontario)

1973
Richelieu Valley Golf
and Country Club
(Ste. Julie de Vercheres, Quebec)

1972
Cherry Hill Club
(Ridgeway, Ontario)

1971
Richelieu Valley Golf
and Country Club
(Ste. Julie de Vercheres, Quebec)

1970
London Hunt
and Country Club
(London, Ontario)

1969
Pine Grove Golf
and Country Club
(St. Luc, Quebec)

1968
St. George's Golf
and Country Club
(Toronto, Ontario)

1967
Montreal Municipal
Golf Course
(Montreal, Quebec)

1966
Shaughnessy Golf
and Country Club
(Vancouver, British Columbia)

1965
Mississaugua Golf
and Country Club
(Mississauga, Ontario)

1964
Pine Grove Golf
and Country Club
(St. Luc, Quebec)

1963
Scarboro Golf
and Country Club
(Scarborough, Ontario)

1962
Le Club Laval-sur-le-Lac
(Laval-sur-le-Lac, Quebec)

1961
Niakwa Country Club
(Winnipeg, Manitoba)

1960
St. George's Golf
and Country Club
(Toronto, Ontario)

1959
Islesmere Golf
and Country Club
(Montreal, Quebec)

1958
Mayfair Golf and Country Club
(Edmonton, Alberta)

1957
Westmount Golf
and Country Club
(Kitchener, Ontario)

1956
Beaconsfield Golf Club
(Pointe-Claire, Quebec)

1955
Weston Golf and Country Club
(Toronto, Ontario)

1954
Point Grey Golf Club
(Vancouver, British Columbia)

1953
Scarboro Golf
and Country Club
(Scarborough, Ontario)

1952
St. Charles Country Club
(Winnipeg, Manitoba)

1951
Mississaugua Golf
and Country Club
(Mississauga, Ontario)

1950
Royal Montreal Golf Club
(Dixie, Quebec)

1949
St. George's Golf
and Country Club
(Toronto, Ontario)

1948
Shaughnessy Heights
Golf Course,
now called Shaughnessy
Golf and Country Club
(Vancouver, British Columbia)

1947
Scarboro Golf
and Country Club
(Scarborough, Ontario)

1946
Beaconsfield Golf Club
(Pointe-Claire, Quebec)

1945
Thornhill Golf Club
(Thornhill, Ontario)

1943—44
Not played due to World War II

1942
Craig Wood Mississaugua
Golf and Country Club
(Mississauga, Ontario)

1941
Lambton Golf Club
(Toronto, Ontario)

1940
Scarboro Golf
and Country Club
(Scarborough, Ontario)

1939
Riverside Country Club
(Saint John, New Brunswick)

1938
Mississaugua Golf
and Country Club
(Mississauga, Ontario)

1937
St. Andrews Club
(Toronto, Ontario)

1936
St. Andrews Golf Club
(Toronto, Ontario)

1935
Summerlea Golf
and Country Club
(Vaudreuil-Dorion, Quebec)

1934
Lakeview Golf Club
(Mississauga, Ontario)

1933
Royal York Golf Club,
now called St. George's Golf
and Country Club
(Toronto, Ontario)

1932
Ottawa Hunt Club
(Ottawa, Ontario)

1931
Mississaugua Golf
and Country Club
(Mississauga, Ontario)

1930
Hamilton Golf and Country Club
(Ancaster, Ontario)

1929
Kanawaki Golf Club
(Kanawaki, Quebec)

1928
Rosedale Golf Club
(Toronto, Ontario)

1927
The Toronto Golf Club
(Mississauga, Ontario)

1926
Royal Montreal Golf Club
(Dixie, Quebec)

1925
Lambton Golf Club
(Toronto, Ontario)

1924
Mt. Bruno Golf Club
(St. Bruno, Quebec)

1923
Lakeview Golf Club
(Mississauga, Ontario)

1922
Mt. Bruno Golf Club
(St. Bruno, Quebec)

1921
The Toronto Golf Club
(Mississauga, Ontario)

1920
Rivermead Golf Club
(Aylmer, Quebec)

1919
Hamilton Golf and Country Club
(Ancaster, Ontario)

1915—18
Not played due to World War I

1914
The Toronto Golf Club
(Mississauga, Ontario)

1913
Royal Montreal Golf Club
(Dixie, Quebec)

1912
Rosedale Golf Club
(Toronto, Ontario)

1911
Royal Ottawa Golf Club
(Aylmer, Quebec)

1910
Lambton Golf Club
(Toronto, Ontario)

1909
The Toronto Golf Club
(Toronto, Ontario)

1908
Royal Montreal Golf Club
(Dixie, Quebec)

1907
Lambton Golf Club
(Toronto, Ontario)

1906
Royal Ottawa Golf Club
(Aylmer, Quebec)

1905
The Toronto Golf Club
(Toronto, Ontario)

1904
Royal Montreal Golf Club
(Dixie, Quebec)

THE AUSTRALIAN OPEN

⌣ The Australian Open was first played in 1904.

⌣ Golf Australia usually holds the tournament in November.

⌣ The winner of the Australian Open receives the Stonehaven Cup.

⌣ The Australian Open is played at the Australian Golf Club, Rosebery, New South Wales, Australia.

Host Courses of the Australian Open

2007
The Australian Golf Club
(Rosebery, New South Wales)

2006
The Royal Sydney Golf Club
(Sydney, New South Wales)

2005
Moonah Links
(Rye, Victoria)

2004
The Australian Golf Club
(Rosebery, New South Wales)

2003
Moonah Links
(Rye, Victoria)

2002
Victoria Golf Club
(Cheltenham, Victoria)

2001
The Grand Golf Club
(Gilston, Queensland)

2000
Kingston Heath Golf Club
(Cheltenham, Victoria)

1999
The Royal Sydney Golf Club
(Sydney, New South Wales)

1998
Royal Adelaide Golf Club
(Seaton, South Australia)

1997
The Metropolitan Golf Club
(Oakleigh, Victoria)

1996
The Australian Golf Club
(Rosebery, New South Wales)

1995
Kingston Heath Golf Club
(Cheltenham, Victoria)

1994
The Royal Sydney Golf Club
(Sydney, New South Wales)

1993
The Metropolitan Golf Club
(Oakleigh, Victoria)

1992
The Lakes Golf Club
(Mascot, New South Wales)

1991
The Royal Melbourne Golf Club
(Melbourne, Victoria)

1990
The Australian Golf Club
(Rosebery, New South Wales)

Multiple winners of the Australian Open

As of the 2006 event the following golfers have won the Australian Open more than once.

7 wins:

Gary Player: 1958, 1962, 1963, 1965, 1969, 1970, 1974

6 wins:

Jack Nicklaus: 1964, 1968, 1971, 1975, 1976, 1978

5 wins:

Greg Norman: 1980, 1985, 1987, 1995, 1996

Ivo Whitton *(amateur)*: 1912, 1913, 1926, 1929, 1931

4 wins:

Ossie Pickworth: 1946, 1947, 1948, 1954

3 wins:

Peter Thomson: 1951, 1967, 1972

Norman Von Nida: 1950, 1952, 1953

C. Clark: 1906, 1910, 1911

2 wins:

Robert Allenby: 1994, 2005

Peter Lonard: 2003, 2004

Aaron Baddeley *(first win as amateur)*: 1999, 2000

Frank Phillips: 1957, 1961

J. B. Ferrier: 1935, 1938

Fred Popplewell: 1925, 1928

Hon. Michael Scott *(amateur)*: 1904, 1907

10 DREAM COURSES

United States

Pebble Beach Golf Links
(Pebble Beach, California)

Pinehurst Resort, Course No. 2
(Village of Pinehurst, North Carolina)

Bandon Dunes Golf Resort, Pacific Dunes Course
(Bandon, Oregon)

Whistling Straits Country Club
(Kohler, Wisconsin)

Bethpage State Park, Black Course
(Farmingdale, New York)

The Players Club at Sawgrass
(Ponte Vedra Beach, Florida)

Canada

Highland Links
(Ingonish, Cape Breton)

Australia

The Royal Melbourne Golf Club
(Melbourne, Victoria)

United Kingdom

St. Andrews
(St. Andrews, Fife, Scotland)

Lahinch Golf Club
(Lahnich, County Clare, Ireland)

GOLF
BASICS

GOLF ORIGINS

★ The game of golf, as we know it today, originated in Scotland. The earliest document referring to golf is the Scottish Act of Parliament in 1457. King James II banned the game because he didn't want it to distract people from practicing archery. The ban wasn't successful. The Scots continued to play their favorite game anyway.

☆ The forerunner of golf is still a mystery. Early club-and-ball games include the Roman game paganica, the French game *jeu de mail*, and the Dutch game *kloven*. However, none of these games feature a hole.

☆ The leather ball stuffed with feathers in paganica is similar to the feathery, a 17th-century golf ball. The fragile and expensive feathery was replaced with the rubberlike gutta percha ball or "guttie". With cheaper balls, golf was no longer just a game for the rich.

☆ Amateur golfer Coburn Haskell invented the rubber-core ball in 1898. He produced it commercially in 1901. Lengths of rubber were wound around a solid core to create a ball with extra spring.

☆ Players used wooden clubs with long noses from the 15th century through the late 19th century.

☆ Golf bags were first bought in the late 1800s. It was a nice change from carrying them under the arm.

☆ Caddie comes from the French cadet, a young man who served in the armed forces or at court. Caddies not only carried golf clubs but would help the player choose the appropriate club and tee up the ball. Caddies have probably existed since the earliest days of golf.

☆ Early courses lacked distinct teeing grounds. Players would shape the sand from the previous hole into a cone. Later in the 18th century, iron sandboxes containing sand for cones were available. In the early 1900s, players could buy celluloid tees. They were sturdy and inexpensive.

PAR TERMINOLOGY

Term on a scoreboard	Definition	Specific Term
- 4	Condor or Vulture *(or triple-eagle)*	four strokes under par
- 3	Albatross *(or double-eagle)*	three strokes under par
- 2	Eagle *(or double-birdie)*	two strokes under par
- 1	Birdie	one stroke under par
0	Par	strokes equal to par
+ 1	Bogey	one stroke more than par
+ 2	Double Bogey	two strokes over par
+ 3	Triple Bogey	three strokes over par

Snowman: Score of 8 shots at a single hole.
(The number "8" resembles the image of a snowman.)

SHOT TERMINOLOGY

Hook:

For a right-handed player, the ball flight starts going right but then curves severely to the left. It's the reverse for a left-handed player. A severe hook is commonly called a duck hook or a snap hook.

Slice:

The ball is left of the target and then curves sharply to the right for a right-handed player, like the shape of a banana. For beginning golfers this is the typical outcome of most shots. A severe slice is commonly referred to as a banana slice or a banana ball.

Pull:

For a right-handed player, the ball is "pulled" across the body and flies to the left of the intended target and heads straight. A pull hook is when the ball starts out left of the target and curves even further to the left. A pull slice is when the ball starts out left then curves back to the right.

Push:

For a right-handed player, the ball is "pushed" away from the body and flies to the right of the intended target. It's the opposite of a pull. A push slice is when the ball starts out right of the target and then curves even further to the right. A push hook is when the ball starts out right and then curves back to the left.

Shank or Lateral:

This is a mis-hit. Instead of hitting the ball on the clubface, the player strikes the ball on the hosel or the outer edge of the club. As a result, for a right-handed player, the ball shoots sharply to the right.

Thin or Blade or Skull:

The player strikes the ball with the bottom edge of the club and not its face. The player's hands may feel some vibration. Often a mis-hit for beginners, this low shot covers a long distance.

Fat or Chunk:

Definitely a mis-hit! The player strikes the ground with his club before hitting the ball. It makes for a short shot and too much turf.

Top:

The player jots the topside of the ball with the blade of the club causing the ball to roll forward on the ground with lots of topspin.

Skyball or Pop-Up:

When the player tees the ball up too high, he strikes the bottom of the ball with the top side of the club. The skyball pops up in the air and only travels a short distance. It's also called "pulling a ty-ty". It's the opposite of a top, but both are mis-hits.

Double-Hit:

The player hits the ball twice in one swing, usually in chipping or pitching. A double-hit is extremely rare in any other kind of shot. Sometimes a double-hit is called a "T. C. Chen" in reference to the Taiwanese golfer who had a five shot lead on Sunday in the 1985 U.S. Open. Chen double-hit a chip shot on the 5th hole and made an eight. This mis-hit cost him the championship.

Flyer or Shooter:

When the golfer doesn't apply enough backspin, the ball will fly through the air and overshoot the target by 10 or more yards.

Hooding the Club:

To lean forward so that the clubface becomes more perpendicular to the ground causing the ball to fly lower to the ground. Hooding the club also creates topspin in a putt.

Wormburner or Groundhog Killer:

The ball is hit extremely low to the ground. It travels quickly across the ground. Watch out, worms and groundhogs!

Foot Wedge:

When a cheater kicks his ball to a better spot. For example, Judge Smails does this in the 1980 film *Caddyshack*.

Whiff or Air Shot:

The player swings and misses the ball. Oh, that was just a practice swing.

Iron Hooker:

When the player leans the club too far forward and flicks the ball. This creates a hook.

Gunnell or Top:

When the player hit the top of the ball with his clubface. This low shot only goes three quarters of the intended distance. In England, golfers would say, "It's a runner, but not a looker". The term "gunnell" is named after the former Olympic hurdler Sally Gunnell.

GREAT INSIGHTS into GOLF

ANGER

They throw their clubs backwards,
and that's wrong.
You should always throw a club
ahead of you so that you don't have to
walk any extra distance to get it.

—*Tommy Bolt, about the tempers of modern players*

. . . . .

If profanity had an influence
on the flight of the ball,
the game of golf would be played
far better than it is.

—*Horace G. Hutchinson*

. . . . .

Real golfers, no matter what the provocation,
never strike a caddie with the driver.
The sand wedge is far more effective.

—*Huxtable Pippey*

. . . . .

Man blames fate for other accidents but feels
personally responsible for a hole in one.

—*Martha Beckman*

They call it golf because all of the other
four-letter words were taken.

—*Raymond Floyd*

. . . . .

I just hope I don't have to explain
all the times I've used
His name in vain when I get up there.

—*Bob Hope, about his golfing*

. . . . .

Have you ever noticed what golf

spells
backwards?

—Al Boliska

THE BALL

Swinging at daisies is like playing electric guitar
with a tennis racket: if it were that easy,
we could all be Jerry Garcia.
The ball changes everything.

—*Michael Bamberger*

. . . . .

If you think it's hard to meet new people,
try picking up the wrong golf ball.

—*Jack Lemmon*

. . . . .

You are meant to play the ball as it lies,
a fact that may help to touch on your own
objective approach to life.

—*Grantland Rice*

. . . . .

Talking to a golf ball won't do you any good.
Unless you do it while your opponent is teeing off.

—*Bruce Lansky*

. . . . .

You can't lose an old golf ball.

—*John Willis*

. . . . .

A golf ball is like a clock. Always hit it at 6 o'clock
and make it go toward 12 o'clock.
But make sure you're in the same time zone.

—*Chi Chi Rodriguez*

. . . . .

It's good sportsmanship not to pick up lost balls
while they are still rolling.

—*Mark Twain*

. . . . .

Don't be in such a hurry. That little white ball
isn't going to run away from you.

—*Patty Berg*

. . . . .

One of the advantages bowling has over golf
is that you seldom lose a bowling ball.

—*Don Carter*

. . . . .

BETTING

Never bet with anyone you meet on the first tee,
who has a deep suntan,
a one iron in his bag and squinty eyes.

—Dave Marr

· · · · ·

You don't know what pressure is until you play
for five bucks with only two bucks in your pocket.

—Lee Trevino

· · · · ·

CADDIES
AND CARTS

My game is so bad I gotta hire three caddies—
one to walk the left rough, one for the right,
and one for the middle. And the one in the middle
doesn't have much to do.

—Dave Hill

. . . . .

If your caddie coaches you on the tee,
"Hit it down the left side with a little draw,"
ignore him. All you do on the tee is try
not to hit the caddie.

—Jim Murray

. . . . .

Many a golfer prefers a golf cart to a caddy
because the cart cannot count, criticize or laugh.

—Anonymous

. . . . .

He who has the fastest golf cart never has a bad lie.

—Mickey Mantle

. . . . .

THE
CLUBHOUSE

All I've got against it is that it takes you
so far from the clubhouse.

—*Eric Linklater*

. . . . .

CLUB PRO

The reason the pro tells you to keep your head down
is so you can't see him laughing.

—*Phyllis Diller*

. . . . .

CLUBS

Actually, the only time I ever took out
a one-iron was to kill a tarantula.
And it took a seven to do that.

—Jim Murray

. . . . .

If you're caught on a golf course during a storm
and are afraid of lightning, hold up a 1-iron.
Not even God can hit a 1-iron.

—Lee Trevino

. . . . .

The worst club in my bag is my brain.

—Chris Perry

. . . . .

The trouble that most of us find with
the modern matched sets of clubs is that
they don't really seem to know any more
about the game than the old ones did.

—Robert Browning

. . . . .

DRIVES

Through years of experience I have found
that air offers less resistance than dirt.

—*Jack Nicklaus, on why he tees his ball high.*

. . . . .

What other people may find in poetry
or art museums, I find in the flight of a good drive.

—*Arnold Palmer*

EXERCISE

Exercise? I get it on the golf course. When I see
my friends collapse, I run for the paramedics.

—*Red Skelton*

FATHERS
AND GOLF

The place of the father in the modern suburban family
is a very small one, particularly if he plays golf.

—*Bertrand Russell*

GOD AND GOLF

The only time my prayers are never answered
is on the golf course.

—*Billy Graham*

. . . . .

If I'm on the course and lightning starts,
I get inside fast. If God wants to play through, let him.

—*Bob Hope*

. . . . .

If you call on God to improve the results of a shot
while it is still in motion, you are using "an outside agency"
and subject to appropriate penalties under the rules of golf.

—*Henry Longhurst*

. . . . .

There are two things you can do with your head down—
play golf and pray.

—*Lee Trevino*

. . . . .

Always keep in mind that if God didn't want a man to have
mulligans, golf balls wouldn't come three to a sleeve.

—*Dan Jenkins*

GOLF COURSES

A golf course is nothing but a poolroom moved outdoors.

—*Barry Fitzgerald*

GOLF FASHION

"Play it as it lies" is one of the fundamental dictates of golf. The other is "Wear it if it clashes."

—*Henry Beard*, Golfing

.　.　.　.　.

You can't call it a sport. You don't run, jump, you don't shoot, you don't pass. All you have to do is buy some clothes that don't match.

—*Steve Sax*

.　.　.　.　.

Hockey is a sport for white men. Basketball is a sport for black men. Golf is a sport for white men dressed like black pimps.

—*Tiger Woods*

.　.　.　.　.

The reason most people play golf is to wear clothes they would not be caught dead in otherwise.

—*Roger Simon*

GOLF ON TELEVISION

Who watches golf on TV?
Who calls eight friends over and gets a keg of beer?
Landscapers, I guess. They sit around the TV, yelling,
"Will you look at that golf path? Pure pea gravel."

—Jeff Cesario

. . . . .

One almost expects one of the players to peer
into the monitor and politely request viewers
to refrain from munching so loudly on cheese and crackers
while the golfers are trying to reach the greens.

—Pete Alfano

. . . . .

There is one thing in this world that is dumber than playing
golf. That is watching someone else playing golf. What do
you actually get to see? Thirty-seven guys in polyester slacks
squinting at the sun. Doesn't that set your blood racing?

—Peter Andrews

. . . . .

I don't like watching golf on TV. I can't stand whispering.

—David Brenner

Anyone who watches golf on television would enjoy
watching the grass grow on the greens.

—*Andy Rooney*

. . . . .

If you want to take long walks,
take long walks. If you want to hit things with sticks,
hit things with sticks. But there's no excuse
for combining the two and putting the results on TV.
Golf is not so much a sport as an insult to lawns.

—National Lampoon

GOLF WIDOWS

When I die, bury me on the golf course
so my husband will visit.

—*Anonymous*

. . . . .

Golf is played by twenty million mature American men
whose wives think they are out having fun.

—*Jim Bishop*

LEGS

The uglier a man's legs are, the better he plays golf.
It's almost a law.

—*H. G. Wells*

LOVE OF GOLF

The ardent golfer would play Mount Everest if somebody put a
flagstick on top.

—*Pete Dye*

. . . . .

Some of us worship in churches, some in synagogues, some on
golf courses.

—*Adlai Stevenson*

. . . . .

I'd play every day if I could. It's cheaper than a shrink and there
are no telephones on my golf cart.

—*Brent Musburger*

. . . . .

Golf may be a hussy, but I love her.

—*Don Herold*

Golf is the most fun you can have
without taking your clothes off.
—Chi Chi Rodriguez

· · · · ·

If you watch a game, it's fun. If you play it, it's recreation.
If you work at it, it's golf.
—Bob Hope

· · · · ·

Golf is like an 18-year-old girl with big boobs.
You know it's wrong but you can't keep away from her.
—Val Doonican

· · · · ·

Don't play too much golf. Two rounds a day are plenty.
—Harry Vardon

· · · · ·

I'm a golfaholic, no question about that.
Counseling wouldn't help me.
They'd have to put me in prison,
and then I'd talk the warden into building
a hole or two and teach him how to play.
—Lee Trevino

· · · · ·

Golf is not just an exercise; it's an adventure,
a romance… a Shakespeare play in which disaster
and comedy are intertwined.

—*Harold Segall*

.　.　.　.　.

An interesting thing about golf is that no matter
how badly you play, it is always possible to get worse.

—*Anonymous*

.　.　.　.　.

One minute you're bleeding. The next minute
you're hemorrhaging. The next minute you're
painting the Mona Lisa.

—*Mac O'Grady, describing a typical round of golf*

.　.　.　.　.

Golf is not a game, it's bondage. It was obviously devised by a
man torn with guilt, eager to atone for his sins.

—*Jim Murray*

.　.　.　.　.

Golf is golf. You hit the ball, you go find it.
Then you hit it again.

—*Lon Hinkle*

.　.　.　.　.

Golf is the cruelest game, because eventually
it will drag you out in front of the whole school,
take your lunch money and slap you around.

—*Rick Reilly*

. . . . .

Golf is the cruelest of sports. Like life, it's unfair.
It's a harlot. A trollop. It leads you on.
It never lives up to its promises....
It's a boulevard of broken dreams. It plays with men.
And runs off with the butcher.

—*Jim Murray*

. . . . .

Golf is essentially an exercise in masochism
conducted out-of-doors.

—*Paul O'Neil*

. . . . .

I regard golf as an expensive way of playing marbles.

—*G. K. Chesterton*

. . . . .

[Golf] is like chasing a quinine pill around a cow pasture.

—*Winston Churchill*

. . . . .

It's easy to see golf not as a game at all but as some whey-faced, nineteenth-century Presbyterian minister's fever dream of exorcism achieved through ritual and self-mortification.

—Bruce McCall

. . . . .

Golf appeals to the idiot in us and the child.
Just how childlike golf players become is proven by their frequent inability to count past five.

—John Updike

. . . . .

A game in which you claim the privileges of age, and retain the playthings of childhood.

—Anonymous, plagiarized from the Samuel Johnson quotation "It is a hopeless endeavour to unite the contrarieties of spring and winter; it is unjust to claim the priveleges of age, and retain the play-things of childhood."

. . . . .

Golf combines two favorite American pastimes: taking long walks and hitting things with a stick.

—P. J. O'Rourke

. . . . .

It is almost impossible to remember how tragic a place this world is when one is playing golf.

—Robert Lynd

113

Golf is so popular simply because it is
the best game in the world at which to be bad.

—*A. A. Milne*

. . . . .

Golf, like the measles, should be caught young,
for, if postponed to riper years,
the results may be serious.

—*P. G. Wodehouse*

. . . . .

Golf is like a love affair.
If you don't take it seriously, it's no fun;
if you do take it seriously, it breaks your heart.

—*Arthur Daley*

. . . . .

Golf is a fascinating game.
It has taken me nearly forty years
to discover that I can't play it.

—*Ted Ray*

. . . . .

I'm the worst golfer in the world and the worst singer
in the world and I love both of those.
Maybe I should sing while I'm playing golf.

—*Jamie Farr*

MIND GAMES

Golf is a game that is played on a five-inch course—
the distance between your ears.

—*Bobby Jones*

. . . . .

I'm about five inches from being an outstanding golfer.
That's the distance my left ear is from my right.

—*Ben Crenshaw*

. . . . .

MULLIGANS

Mulligan: invented by an Irishman who wanted to hit
one more twenty yard grounder.

—*Jim Bishop*

ON THE TOUR

After all these years, it's still embarrassing
for me to play on the American golf tour.
Like the time I asked my caddie
for a sand wedge and he came back
ten minutes later with a ham on rye.

—*Chi Chi Rodriguez, on his Puerto Rican accent*

. . . . .

What's nice about our tour is you
can't remember your bad shots.

—*Bob Bruce, about the senior tour*

. . . . .

POLITICS

In golf, you keep your head down and follow through.
In the vice presidency, you keep your head up
and follow through. It's a big difference.

—*Dan Quayle*

PRESIDENTS
AND ROYALTY

Golf is an ineffectual attempt
to put an elusive ball into an obscure hole
with implements ill-adapted to the purpose.

—Woodrow Wilson

. . . . .

Show me a man who plays a good game of golf
and I'll show you a man who is neglecting something.

—John F. Kennedy

. . . . .

As if we don't have enough violence on television.

*—Barbara Bush, First Lady, after her husband accidentally hit two
spectators with golf balls during a celebrity golf tournament, 1995.*

. . . . .

Congress.

*—Lyndon B. Johnson,
while visiting the Masters golf tournament
was asked by a spectator what his handicap was.*

. . . . .

Golf seems to me an arduous way to go for a walk.
I prefer to take the dogs out.

—*Princess Anne of Great Britain*

. . . . .

The great thing about this game
is that the bad days are wonderful.

—*Bill Clinton*

. . . . .

One lesson you better learn
if you want to be in politics is that
you never go out on a golf course
and beat the President.

—*Lyndon B. Johnson*

PUTTING

If you drink, don't drive. Don't even putt.

—Dean Martin

. . . . .

Even God has to practice his putting.

—Golf Saying

. . . . .

That son of a bitch was able to hole a putt
over 60 feet of peanut brittle.

—Lloyd Mangrum, about Bobby Locke

. . . . .

The least thing upset him on the links.
He missed short putts because of the uproar
of butterflies in the adjoining meadows.

—P. G. Wodehouse

. . . . .

It's so bad I could putt off a tabletop and
still leave the ball halfway down the leg.

—J. C. Snead, on his putting

Happiness
is a
long walk

with a putter.

—Greg Norman

I never pray to God to make a putt.
I pray to God to help me react good if I miss a putt.

—*Chi Chi Rodriguez*

. . . . .

Why am I using a new putter?
Because the last one didn't float too well.

—*Craig Stadler*

. . . . .

Putts get real difficult the day they hand out the money.

—*Lee Trevino*

. . . . .

There are no points for style when it comes to putting.
It's getting the ball in the cup that counts.

—*Brian Swarbrick*

. . . . .

Yeah, after each of my downhill putts.

—*Homero Blancas, asked if he had any uphill putts*

. . . . .

The game of golf would lose a great deal if croquet mallets and
billiard cues were allowed on the putting green.

—*Ernest Hemingway*

These greens are so fast I have to hold my putter
over the ball and hit it with the shadow.

—*Sam Snead*

. . . . .

Is my friend in the bunker or is the bastard on the green?

—*Anonymous*

. . . . .

There's an old saying,
"It's a poor craftsman who blames his tools."
It's usually the player who misses those three-footers,
not the putter.

—*Kathy Whitworth*

. . . . .

When I putt, my emotions collide like tectonic plates.
It's left my memory circuits full of scars that won't heal.

—*Mac O'Grady*

. . . . .

Find a man with both feet firmly on the ground
and you've found a man about to make a difficult putt.

—*Fletcher Knebel*

. . . . .

A "gimme" can best be defined as an agreement between
two golfers, neither of whom can putt very well.

—*Anonymous*

. . . . .

Golf is a day spent in a round of strenuous idleness.

—*William Wordsworth*

. . . . .

RETIREMENT

Baseball players quit playing and they take up golf.
Basketball players quit, take up golf.
Football players quit, take up golf.
What are we supposed to take up when we quit?

—*George Archer*

. . . . .

Every rock'n'roll band I know,
guys with long hair and tattoos, plays golf now.

—*Alice Cooper*

SAND TRAPS, WATER, AND OTHER HAZARDS

If your opponent is playing several shots
in vain attempts to extricate himself from a bunker,
do not stand near him and audibly count his strokes.
It would be justifiable homicide if he wound up his pitiable
exhibition by applying his niblick to your head.

—Harry Vardon

. . . . .

One under a tree, one under a bush, one under the water.

*—Lee Trevino, describing how he was one under
during a tournament*

. . . . .

A passion, an obsession, a romance,
a nice acquaintanceship with trees, sand, and water.

—Bob Ryan

. . . . .

125

You know what they say about big hitters…
the woods are full of them.

—*Jimmy Demaret*

. . . . .

Golf balls are attracted to water as unerringly
as the eye of a middle-aged man to a female bosom.

—*Michael Green*

. . . . .

I'm hitting the woods just great,
but I'm having a terrible time getting out of them.

—*Harry Toscano*

. . . . .

I know I am getting better at golf because
I'm hitting fewer spectators.

—*Gerald Ford*

. . . . .

I can airmail the golf ball, but sometimes
I don't put the right address on it.

—*Jim Dent*

. . . . .

I tried real hard to play golf,
and I was so bad at it they would have to
check me for ticks at the end of the round
because I'd spent about half the day in the woods.

—Jeff Foxworthy

.   .   .   .   .

Drugs are very much a part of professional sports today,
but when you think about it, golf is the only sport where the
players aren't penalized for being on grass.

—Bob Hope

.   .   .   .   .

I would like to deny all allegations by Bob Hope
that during my last game of golf, I hit an eagle,
a birdie, an elk and a moose.

—Gerald Ford

SCORES

I have a tip that can take five strokes off
anyone's golf game: it's called an eraser.

—Arnold Palmer

. . . . .

It took me seventeen years to get 3,000 hits.
I did it in one afternoon on the golf course.

—Hank Aaron

. . . . .

Golf is a game in which you yell "fore,"
shoot six, and write down five.

—Paul Harvey

. . . . .

I'll shoot my age if I have to live to be 105.

—Bob Hope

. . . . .

To some golfers, the greatest handicap
is the ability to add correctly.

—Anonymous

My best score ever was 103,
but I've only been playing 15 years.

—*Alex Karris*

. . . . .

Golf is the hardest game in the world to play,
and the easiest to cheat at.

—*Dave Hill*

. . . . .

I play in the low 80s.
If it's any hotter than that, I won't play.

—*Joe E. Lewis*

. . . . .

If you pick up a golfer and hold it close to your ear,
like a conch shell, and listen—you will hear an alibi.

—*Fred Beck*

. . . . .

Golf is a game in which the ball lies poorly
and the players well.

—*Art Rosenbaum*

. . . . .

I'll always remember the day I broke ninety.
I had a few beers in the clubhouse and was so excited
I forgot to play the back nine.

—*Bruce Lansky*

. . . . .

The best wood in most amateurs' bags is the pencil.

—*Anonymous*

. . . . .

Any game where a man 60 can beat a man 30 ain't no game.

—*Burt Shotton*

. . . . .

The first time I played the Masters,
I was so nervous I drank a bottle of rum
before I teed off. I shot the happiest 83 of my life.

—*Chi Chi Rodriguez*

. . . . .

The number of shots taken by an opponent
who is out of sight is equal to the square root
of the sum of the number of curses heard
plus the number of swishes.

—*Michael Green*

Columbus went around the world in 1492. That isn't a lot of
strokes when you consider the course.

—*Lee Trevino*

. . . . .

Isn't it fun to go out on the course and lie in the sun?

—*Bob Hope*

. . . . .

If there is any larceny in a man,
golf will bring it out.

—*Paul Gallico*

. . . . .

If you break 100, watch your golf.
If you break 80, watch your business.

—*Joey Adams*

. . . . .

Golf is a lot of walking,
broken up by disappointment and bad arithmetic.

—*Anonymous*

. . . . .

SEX AND GOLF

Golf and sex are the only things you can enjoy
without being good at them.

—Jimmy Demaret

. . . . .

The golf swing is like sex.
You can't be thinking about the mechanics
of the act while you are performing.

—Dave Hill

. . . . .

Golf is more fun than walking naked
in a strange place, but not much.

—Buddy Hackett

. . . . .

SWINGS, SLICES, HOOKS, AND OTHER BAD SHOTS

I'm not saying my golf game went bad,
but if I grew tomatoes, they'd come up sliced.

—Attributed to both Miller Barber and Lee Trevino

. . . . .

Golf is an awkward set of bodily contortions
designed to produce a graceful result.

—Tommy Armour

. . . . .

But you don't have to go up in the stands
and play your foul balls. I do.

—Sam Snead,
to Ted Williams, arguing which was more difficult,
to hit a moving baseball or a stationary golf ball

. . . . .

My handicap?

Woods
and *irons.*

—Chris Codiroli

Duffers who consistently shank their balls
are urged to buy and study *Shanks—
No Thanks* by R. K. Hoffman, or in extreme cases,
M. S. Howard's excellent *Tennis for Beginners.*

—*Henry Beard*, Golfing, *1985*

.   .   .   .   .

You can talk to a fade but a hook won't listen.

—*Lee Trevino*

.   .   .   .   .

Art said he wanted to get more distance.
I told him to hit it and run backward.

—*Ken Venturi, on Art Rosenbaum*

.   .   .   .   .

If I hit it right, it's a slice. If I hit it left, it's a hook.
If I hit it straight, it's a miracle.

—*Anonymous*

.   .   .   .   .

In baseball you hit your home run over the
right-field fence, the left-field fence, the center-field fence.
Nobody cares. In golf everything has got to be
right over second base.

—*Ken Harrelson*

If a lot of people gripped a knife and fork
the way they do a golf club, they'd starve to death.

—*Sam Snead*

．．．．．

Hit 'em hard. They'll land somewhere.

—*Stewart Maiden*

．．．．．

Swing hard in case you hit it.

—*Dan Marino*

．．．．．

My favorite shots are the practice swing
and the conceded putt. The rest can never be mastered.

—*Lord Robertson*

．．．．．

The golf swing is like a suitcase into which
we are trying to pack one too many things.

—*John Updike*

．．．．．

If I can hit a curveball, why can't I hit a ball
that is standing still on a course?

—*Larry Nelson*

137

Grip it and rip it. It works for John Daly.
It never worked for me.
All I did was wear out golf gloves.

—*Chuck Stark*

. . . . .

Obviously a deer on the fairway has seen
you tee off before and knows that the safest place to be
when you play is right down the middle.

—*Jackie Gleason*

. . . . .

Everybody has two swings—
a beautiful practice swing and the choked-up one
with with which they hit the ball. So it wouldn't
do either of us a damned bit of good
to look at your practice swing.

—*Ed Furgol*

. . . . .

My swing is so bad I look like a caveman killing his lunch.

—*Lee Trevino*

. . . . .

One thing about golf is you don't know why
you play bad and why you play good.

—*George Archer*

. . . . .

Nobody ever looked up and saw a good shot.

—*Don Herold*

. . . . .

Golf isn't like other sports where you
can take a player out if he's having a bad day.
You have to play the whole game.

—*Phil Blackmar*

. . . . .

I like trying to win. That's what golf is all about.

—*Jack Nicklaus*

. . . . .

It is more satisfying to be a bad player at golf.
The worse you play, the better you remember
the occasional good shot.

—*Nubar Gulbenkian, 1972*

THE VALUE OF GOLF

If you wish to hide your character, do not play golf.

—Percey Boomer

.　.　.　.　.

Golf is not a game of great shots.
It's a game of the most misses.
The people who win make the smallest mistakes.

—Gene Littler

.　.　.　.　.

Golf is a game not just of manners but of morals.

—Art Spander

.　.　.　.　.

Golf is life. If you can't take golf, you can't take life.

—Anonymous

.　.　.　.　.

Playing the game I have learned the meaning
of humility. It has given me an understanding
of futility of the human effort.

—Abba Eban

Golf is not, on the whole, a game for realists.
By its exactitudes of measurements it invites
the attention of perfectionists.

—*Heywood Hale Broun*

. . . . .

One of the most fascinating things about golf
is how it reflects the cycle of life.
No matter what you shoot—
the next day you have to go back to the first tee
and begin all over again and
make yourself into something.

—*Peter Jacobsen*

. . . . .

Live….Laugh….GOLF!!!

—*Kathryn Schaefer Plaum*

. . . . .

Golf is based on honesty,
where else would you admit to a seven
on a par three?

—*Jimmy Demaret*

. . . . .

Golf
is a
good
walk

spoiled.

—Mark Twain

Eighteen holes of match or medal play
will teach you more about your foe than will
18 years of dealing with him across a desk.

—*Grantland Rice*

. . . . .

Forget your opponents; always play against par.

—*Sam Snead*

. . . . .

I've spent most of my life golfing…
the rest I've just wasted.

—*Anonymous*

. . . . .

The sport of choice for the urban poor is basketball.
The sport of choice for maintenance level employees is bowling.
The sport of choice for front-line workers is football.
The sport of choice for supervisors is baseball.
The sport of choice for middle management is tennis.
The sport of choice for corporate officers is golf.
Conclusion: The higher you are in the corporate structure,
the smaller your balls become.

—*Anonymous*

. . . . .

They say golf is like life, but don't believe them.
Golf is more complicated than that.

—*Gardner Dickinson*

. . . . .

There's no game like golf: you go out with three friends,
play eighteen holes, and return with three enemies.

—*Anonymous*

. . . . .

I guess there is nothing that will get your mind
off everything like golf. I have never been depressed enough
to take up the game, but they say you get so sore at yourself
you forget to hate your enemies.

—*Will Rogers*

. . . . .

Golf is an open exhibition of overweening ambition, courage
deflated by stupidity, skill scoured by a whiff of arrogance.

—*Alistair Cooke*

. . . . .

No game designed to be played with the aid of
personal servants by right-handed men who can't even bring
along their dogs can be entirely good for the soul.

—*Bruce McCall, "The Case Against Golf,"* Esquire

WOMEN
AND GOLF

Give me the fresh air, a beautiful partner,
and a nice round of golf, and you can keep
the fresh air and the round of golf.

—Jack Benny

. . . . .

WOMEN
ON GOLF

"After all, golf is only a game," said Millicent.
Women say these things without thinking.
It does not mean that there is a kink in their character.
They simply don't realise what they are saying.

—P. G. Wodehouse, Order by Golf, *1922*

. . . . .

12

☆ of the ☆

WORLD'S MOST FAMOUS GOLFERS PAST and PRESENT

JACK NICKLAUS

Birth: January 21, 1940
Turned professional in 1961
Professional Wins: 113

Major Championships

- Wins: 18

- Masters: (6 wins) 1963, 1965, 1966, 1972, 1975, 1986

- U.S. Open: (4 wins) 1962, 1967, 1972, 1980

- The Open Championship: (3 wins) 1966, 1970, 1978

- PGA Championship: (5 wins) 1963, 1971, 1973, 1975, 1980

Amazing Records

- In 1963, at the age of 23, he was the youngest player to win the Masters. He held this record until Tiger Woods won in 2005.

- Nicklaus won the 1962 U.S. Open, the 1963 Masters, and the 1963 PGA Championship in 18 months.

◡ After his 1966 Masters victory, he became the first golfer to win two consecutive Masters.

◡ Over four days in the 1980 U.S. Open, he trumped his 1967 U.S. Open score with a new total of 272.

◡ Nicklaus won a career Grand Slam (all 4 majors). Sarazen, Player, Hogan, and Woods have also won career Grand Slams.

Fascinating Trivia

◡ Nicklaus was first introduced to golf when he accompanied his father, who was recovering from a broken bone in his ankle. Jack started playing golf at the age of 10.

◡ He won his first U.S. Amateur in 1959.

◡ Nicklaus's nickname is the "Golden Bear".

◡ He made 20 holes-in-one during 1962 through 2003.

◡ In 1974, Nicklaus became one of the 13 original inductees into the World Golf Hall of Fame.

◡ *Sports Illustrated* honored Nicklaus with the title Best Individual Male Athlete of the 20th Century.

Memorable Moments

○ In the 1962 U.S. Open, Nicklaus astonished spectators when he defeated Arnold Palmer by three strokes in the 18-hole play-off.

○ Nicklaus's 12-foot birdie at the 16th hole helped him win the 1963 Masters.

○ Not only did Nicklaus beat Palmer in the 1965 Masters, but he was 17 strokes under par.

○ Nicklaus's 1-iron from 238 yards at the 72nd hole during the 1967 U.S. Open is the stuff of legends.

○ At the age of 46, he won his sixth Masters in 1986 with a back-nine 30.

ARNOLD PALMER

Birth: September 10, 1929
Turned professional in 1954
Professional Wins: 95

Major Championships

↘ Wins: 7

↘ Masters: (4 wins) 1958, 1960, 1962, 1964

↘ U.S. Open: (1 win) 1960

↘ The Open Championship: (2 wins) 1961, 1962

Amazing Records

↘ Palmer was the first golfer to win the Masters four times. Nicklaus and Woods have also accomplished this feat.

↘ He was one of the first leading U.S. golfers to compete and win in the Open Championship. His victories encouraged other Americans to compete.

↘ Palmer won 29 PGA Tour events during 1960 to 1963.

↘ Palmer was the first golfer to earn $1 million on the PGA Tour.

Fascinating Trivia

↘ Palmer's nickname is "The King".

↘ His loyal fans on the course were called "Arnie's Army".

↘ Palmer's charm, his dynamic skills, and the advent of television in the 1950s helped make him a household name.

↘ A drink was even named after him! "The Original Arnold Palmer Tee" consists of half lemonade and half iced tea.

↘ In 1974, Palmer became one of the 13 original inductees into the World Golf Hall of Fame.

↘ Palmer won the PGA Tour Lifetime Achievement Award in 1998.

Memorable Moments

In the 1960 Masters, Palmer shot birdies on the final two holes and defeated Ken Venturi.

Palmer won the 1960 U.S. Open with a score of 65 in the final round and seven strokes out of the lead. It was a dazzling comeback!

In 1961, Palmer won the Open Championship by one stroke.

GARY PLAYER

Birth: November 1, 1935
Turned professional in 1953
Professional Wins: 163

Major Championships

▶ Wins: 9

▶ Masters: (3 wins) 1961, 1974, 1978

▶ U.S. Open : (1 win) 1965

▶ The Open Championship: (3 wins) 1959, 1968, 1974

▶ PGA Championship: (2 wins) 1962, 1972

Amazing Records

▶ In 1959, Player (age 23) was the youngest golfer to win the Open Championship.

▶ In 1965, at the age of 29, Player was the third golfer to win a career Grand Slam.

▷ Player also was the second player from South Africa, after Bobby Locke, to win the majors multiple times.

▷ Player is the only 20th-century golfer to have won the Open Championship in three different decades.

Fascinating Trivia

▷ Player was born in Johannesburg, South Africa.

▷ Player is also an internationally renowned architect. He has designed over 250 golf courses.

▷ He earned his nickname "The Black Knight" because he always dresses in his lucky color, black.

▷ Player, Nicklaus, and Palmer were called "The Big Three".

▷ In 1966, the United States Golf Association honored Player with the Bob Jones Award.

▷ In 1974, Player became one of the 13 original inductees into the World Golf Hall of Fame.

▷ He has traveled over 14 million miles—more than any other athlete in history.

Memorable Moments

▶ In 1961, Player defeated Palmer and won the Masters with an 8-under 280.

▶ Player defeated Bob Goalby in the 1962 PGA Championship by parring the final two rounds.

▶ Player's 1965 win in the U.S. Open secured his career Grand Slam. He won by three strokes in the 18-hole play-off.

TIGER WOODS

Birth: December 30, 1975
Turned professional in 1996
Professional Wins: 83

Major Championships

★ Wins: 13

★ Masters: (4 wins) 1997, 2001, 2002, 2005

★ U.S. Open: (2 wins) 2000, 2002

★ The Open Championship: (3 wins) 2000, 2005, 2006

★ PGA Championship: (4 wins) 1999, 2000, 2006, 2007

Amazing Records

★ In 1997, at age 21, he was the youngest golfer to win the Masters. He won with a 12-stroke lead, the largest victory margin ever in the Masters.

★ Woods achieved a career Gram Slam.

★ After winning the 2001 Masters, Woods held all 4 Major titles at once. This hadn't yet been accomplished in the modern era of golf.

★ Not since Ben Hogan in 1948, had a player won six consecutive tournaments. Woods achieved this feat during 1999 to 2000.

★ He has won the PGA Tour Player of the Year Award eight times—a PGA record.

Fascinating Trivia

★ His first name is Eldrick.

★ He appeared on *The Mike Douglas Show* with Bob Hope when he was 2 years old.

★ In 1997, Woods was the first non-white player to win the Masters.

★ He was the PGA Tour money winner seven times.

★ Both he and Lance Armstrong have been named Associate Press Male Athlete of the Year four times.

Memorable Moments

☆ In the 1997 Masters, Woods won with an amazing score of 270, a 72-hole record.

☆ In the 1999 PGA Championship, Woods defeated Sergio García one stroke ahead.

☆ He won the 2000 Open Championship by eight strokes.

☆ Woods won the 2000 U.S. Open by 15 strokes, breaking Tom Morris, Sr.'s record of 13 strokes at the 1864 Open Championship.

PHIL MICKELSON

Birth: June 16, 1970
Turned professional in 1992
Professional Wins: 37

Major Championships

- Wins: (3)

- Masters: (2 wins) 2004, 2006

- PGA Championship: (1 win) 2005

Amazing Records

- In 1990, Mickelson was the first left-handed player to win the U.S. Amateur.

- After he won the 2006 Masters, Mickelson was second place in the Official World Golf rankings. Woods was ranked number one.

Fascinating Trivia

○ Mickelson earned his nickname "Lefty" for his signature left-handed swing. (Actually, Mickelson is right-handed.)

○ His average for drives is over 285 yards.

○ At age 4, he was already playing full rounds of golf.

○ Up until his 2004 Masters win, he had been labeled as "the best player never to win a major".

○ He has played on six Ryder Cup teams (1995, 1997, 1999, 2002, 2004, and 2006).

○ He wrote a memoir with Donald T. Phillips titled *One Magical Sunday* in 2005.

Memorable Moments

○ In 2004, Mickelson won the Masters with a 20-foot birdie at the final hole.

○ Mickelson won the 2005 PGA Championship with a 4-under-par total of 276.

○ In the 2006 Masters, Mickelson defeated Tim Clark by 2 strokes.

LEE TREVINO

Birth: December 1, 1939
Turned professional in 1960
Professional Wins: 85

Major Championships

\ Wins: 6

\ U.S. Open: (2 wins) 1968, 1971

\ The Open Championship: (2 wins) 1971, 1972

\ PGA Championship: (2 wins) 1974, 1984

Amazing Records

\ In 1968, Trevino was the first player to score under par in all four rounds of the U.S. Open.

\ He was the first Champions Tour player to make more than $1 million in single-season earnings in 1990.

\ Lee Trevino, Bobby Jones, and Gene Sarazen are the only Americans who have won both the Open Championship and the U.S. Open in the same year.

Fascinating Trivia

\ Trevino is a self-taught golfer. His swing has been compared to that of a baseball batter's.

\ He earned the PGA Tour Rookie of the Year award in 1967.

\ At the first hole of the 1971 U.S. Open, Trevino threw out a rubber snake from his bag as a practical joke for Nicklaus.

\ In 1971, he was honored as the *Sports Illustrated* Sportsman of the Year and the Associated Press Male Athlete of the Year.

\ In 1975, Lee Trevino, Bobby Nichols, and Jerry Heard were struck by lightening at the Western Open.

\ Trevino won the Vardon Trophy, an award for the season's lowest scoring average, five times (1970, 1971, 1972, 1974, and 1980).

\ He was inducted into the World Golf Hall of Fame in 1981.

Memorable Moments

\ In the 1968 U.S. Open, Trevino won by 4 strokes. His score was 275.

\ In the 1971 U.S. Open, Trevino defeated Nicklaus in the 18-hole playoff by 3 shots.

\ In 1972, his 30-foot chip shot earned him his second Open Championship win. He beat Nicklaus.

\ Trevino defeated Nicklaus at the 1974 PGA Championship, despite the heavy rain.

GREG NORMAN

Birth: February 10, 1955
Turned professional in 1976
Professional Wins: 87

Major Championships

☆ Wins: 2

☆ The Open Championship: (2 wins) 1986, 1993

Amazing Records

☆ In 1993, Norman's winning score of 267 beat Tom Watson's 1977 record of 268 in the Open Championship.

☆ In 1996, he was the first golfer to earn over $10 million in his career.

Fascinating Trivia

☆ Norman has an aggressive playing style. His nickname is "The Great White Shark".

☆ In 1990, Norman's drive average was 282 yards, whereas other PGA Tour players were averaging 262 yards.

☆ He had eight top-five finishes at the Masters.

☆ Norman was a PGA Tour of Australia Order of Merit Winner six times (1978, 1980, 1983, 1984, 1986, and 1988).

☆ Norman won the Vardon Trophy three times (1989, 1990, and 1994).

☆ In the PGA Tour, he was the leading career money winner by 1995.

☆ Norman was inducted into the World Golf Hall of Fame in 2001.

Memorable Moments

☆ In the 1986 Open Championship, Norman defeated Gordon Brand by five strokes. Norman's total score was 280.

☆ Norman had a two-stroke victory over Nick Faldo at the 1993 Open Championship.

MIKE WEIR

Birth: May 12, 1970
Turned professional in 1992
Professional Wins: 11

Major Championships

▷ Wins: 1

▷ Masters: (1 win) 2003

Amazing Records

▷ His win at the 1999 Air Canada Championship in Surrey, British Columbia was the first time in 45 years that a Canadian had won a PGA Tour event in Canada.

▷ Weir is also the first Canadian to win one of the majors; he won the 2003 Masters.

▷ He is the second left-handed golfer to win one of the majors. Another left-handed player, Bob Charles, won the 1963 Open Championship.

Fascinating Trivia

▷ In 2003, Weir was recognized as outstanding Canadian Athlete of the Year with the Lou Marsh Trophy.

▷ Like Mickelson , he has a left-handed swing, even though he is right-handed.

▷ He was appointed to the Order of Ontario in 2003.

▷ In 2003 and 2004, he was ranked in the top 10 in the PGA Tour.

Memorable Moments

▷ In 2003, Weir won the Masters with a one shot lead. He defeated Len Mattiace. His total score was 281.

▷ He won back-to-back championships at the 2004 Nissan Open. He was the sixth player to accomplish this feat.

BEN HOGAN

Birth: August 13, 1912

Death: July 25, 1997

Turned professional in 1929

Professional Wins: 64

Major Championships

○ Wins: 9

○ Masters: (2 wins) 1951, 1953

○ U.S. Open: (4 wins) 1948, 1950, 1951, 1953

○ The Open Championship: (1 win) 1953

○ PGA Championship: (2 wins) 1946, 1948

Amazing Records

○ Hogan was the first player to win three majors in the same year. He won the Western Open, the National Open, and the U.S. Open.

○ He set a tournament record with a total score of 274 at the 1953 Masters.

○ Hogan won a career Grand Slam.

Fascinating Trivia

○ Ben Hogan and Byron Nelson both caddied at the Glen Garden Country Club.

○ In the late 1930s, Hogan started swinging left-handed.

○ Hogan made an amazing recovery from a car accident. He worked diligently at walking and playing golf. After the accident, he won a total of six championships, including the 1950 U.S. Open.

○ The biographical film *Follow the Sun* (1951) starred Glenn Ford.

○ After his 1953 Open Championship win, Hogan received a ticker-tape parade in New York.

○ He was the PGA Tour money winner five times (1940, 1941, 1942, 1946, and 1948).

○ Hogan was PGA Tour Player of the Year four times (1948, 1950, 1951, and 1953).

○ Hogan won the Vardon Trophy three times (1940, 1941, and 1948).

He wrote *Five Lessons: The Modern Fundamentals of Golf* with Herbert Warren Wind in 1957.

In 1974, Hogan became one of the 13 original inductees into the World Golf Hall of Fame.

Memorable Moments

In the 1950 U.S. Open, Hogan won by four strokes over Lloyd Mangrum and six strokes over George Fazio, despite painful leg cramps.

Hogan defeated Skee Riegel by two strokes in the 1951 Masters.

He beat Clayton Heafner by two strokes in the 1951 U.S. Open.

In the 1953 Masters, Hogan won by five strokes. He defeated Ed Oliver.

He won the 1953 U.S. Open over Sam Snead by 6 strokes.

Hogan won the 1953 Open Championship by 4 strokes over Frank Stranahan and Peter Thomson.

BOBBY JONES

Birth: March 17, 1902

Death: December 18, 1971

Major Championships

↘ Wins: 7

↘ U.S. Open: (4 wins) 1923, 1926, 1929, 1930

↘ The Open Championship: (3 wins) 1926, 1927, 1930

Amateur Majors

↘ (Back then, National Amateurs counted as major championships.)

↘ U.S. Amateur: 1924, 1925, 1927, 1928, 1930

↘ British Amateur: 1930

Amazing Records

↘ Jones was the first player to hold both the U.S. Open and Open Championship titles in one year.

In 1930, Jones was the first golfer to achieve a Grand Slam in one year.

Fascinating Trivia

Jones's hickory putter with a steel head was named "Calamity Jane".

He received two ticker-tape parades in New York, one in 1926 after his British Amateur and British Open victories and another in 1930 after he had achieved his Grand Slam.

Jones played on the first Walker Cup Team in 1922, 1924, 1926, 1928, and 1930. He was captain in 1928 and 1930. The U.S. won all of the contests until 1938.

Jones also wrote a few books: an autobiography called *Down the Fairway* (with O. B. Keeler), *Golf Is My Game*, and *Bobby Jones on Golf*.

Jones and Alister MacKenzie designed the Augusta National course.

He and Cliff Roberts helped found the Masters Tournament.

In 1974, Jones became one of the 13 original inductees into the World Golf Hall of Fame.

Memorable Moments

⟍ In the 1923 U.S. Open, Jones was tied with Bobby Cruickshank. Jones won the 18-hole play-off by 2 strokes.

⟍ He defeated Joe Turnesa in the 1926 U.S. Open by one stroke.

⟍ Jones won the 1926 Open Championship over Al Watrous with a score of 291.

⟍ He won the 1927 Open Championship over Aubrey Boomer by six strokes.

⟍ In the 1929 U.S. Open, Jones beat Al Espinosa in a 36-hole play-off by twenty-three strokes.

⟍ Jones won the 1930 U.S. Open over Macdonald Smith by 2 strokes.

⟍ In the 1930 Open Championship, Jones defeated Leo Diegel and Macdonald Smith. He won by two strokes.

NICK FALDO

Birth: July 18, 1957
Turned professional in 1976
Professional Wins: 43

Major Championships

☆ Wins: 6

☆ Masters: (3 wins) 1989, 1990, 1996

☆ The Open Championship: (3 wins) 1987, 1990, 1992

Amazing Records

☆ Faldo set a record for playing on 11 different Ryder Cup teams (1977, 1979, 1981, 1983, 1985, 1987, 1989, 1991, 1993, 1995, and 1997). He played the most matches (46), won the most points (25), and won the most matches (23).

☆ He won more of the four majors than any other player worldwide during 1987 through 1996. Faldo won 6 major tournaments: 3 Masters and 3 Open Championships.

Fascinating Trivia

☆ In 1977, Faldo earned the title European Rookie of the Year at the age of 20.

☆ Faldo was a top European player during the late 1980s through the early 1990s.

☆ Faldo was the PGA Tour Player of the Year in 1990.

☆ He was inducted into the World Golf Hall of Fame in 1998.

☆ Faldo has been a broadcaster for ABC Sports during the PGA Championships.

☆ In 2006, he became a golf analyst for CBS.

Memorable Moments

☆ In the 1987 Open Championship, Faldo won by one stroke. He beat Paul Azinger and Rodger Davis.

☆ In the 1989 Masters, Faldo had a five shot deficit, but he won the play-off over Scott Hoch.

☆ Faldo won the play-off in the 1990 Masters, beating Raymond Floyd. Faldo had 8; Floyd had 9.

☆ Faldo defeated Mark McNulty and Payne Stewart in the 1990 Open Championship. He won by 5 strokes.

☆ In the 1992 Open Championship, he won over John Cook by 1 stroke.

☆ Faldo won the 1996 Masters with an amazing comeback. Faldo defeated Greg Norman. He was behind six strokes early in the final round. On the 13th, with his 2-iron, he made a stellar clutch shot.

COLIN MONTGOMERIE

Birth: June 23, 1963
Turned professional in 1987
Professional Wins: 39

Major Championships

▷ Montgomerie has never won a major tournament, but he has been a runner-up five times.

Amazing Records

▷ In 1993, Montgomerie was ranked number one on the European money list for a record-breaking number of seven years.

▷ In 2005, he was the first golfer to earn 20 million Euros on the European Tour.

▷ Montgomerie has won 31 European Tour tournaments—more than any other British golfer.

Fascinating Trivia

▷ He was one of the first British golfers to go to college in the United States. He went to Houston Baptist University.

▷ Montgomerie was the European Rookie of the Year in 1988.

▷ Montgomerie played on the European Ryder Cup team eight times (1991, 1993, 1995, 1997, 1999, 2002, 2004, and 2006). He has won all of his singles matches.

▷ He was the European Tour Order of Merit Winner eight times (1993, 1994, 1995, 1996, 1997, 1998, 1999, and 2005).

▷ In 1994, Montgomerie placed in the top 10 of the Official World Golf Rankings.

Memorable Moments

▷ Montgomerie won the 1989 Portuguese Open by 8 strokes.

▷ In the 2004 Ryder Cup match, he made the winning putt.

The Long Hole

BY P. G. WODEHOUSE

The young man, as he sat filling his pipe in the club-house smoking-room, was inclined to be bitter.

"If there's one thing that gives me a pain squarely in the centre of the gizzard," he burst out, breaking a silence that had lasted for some minutes, "it's a golf-lawyer. They oughtn't to be allowed on the links."

The Oldest Member, who had been meditatively putting himself outside a cup of tea and a slice of seed-cake, raised his white eyebrows.

"The Law," he said, "is an honourable profession. Why should its practitioners be restrained from indulgence in the game of games?"

"I don't mean actual lawyers," said the young man, his acerbity mellowing a trifle under the influence of tobacco. "I mean the blighters whose best club is the book of rules. You know the sort of excrescences. Every time you think you've won a hole, they dig out Rule eight hundred and fifty-three, section two, sub-section four, to prove that you've disqualified yourself by having an ingrowing toe-nail. Well, take my case." The young man's voice was high and plaintive. "I go out with that man Hemmingway to play an ordinary friendly round—nothing depending on it except a measly ball—and on the seventh he pulls me up and claims the hole simply because I happened to drop my niblick in the bunker. Oh, well, a tick's a tick, and there's nothing more to say, I suppose."

The Sage shook his head.

"Rules are rules, my boy, and must be kept. It is odd that you should have brought up this subject, for only a moment before you came in I was thinking of a somewhat curious match which ultimately turned upon a question of the rule-book. It is true that, as far as the actual prize was concerned, it made little difference. But perhaps I had better tell you the whole story from the beginning."

The young man shifted uneasily in his chair.

"Well, you know, I've had a pretty rotten time this afternoon already——"

"I will call my story," said the Sage, tranquilly, "'The Long Hole', for it involved the playing of what I am inclined to think must be the longest hole in the history of golf. In its beginnings the story may remind you of one I once told you about Peter Willard and James Todd, but you will find that it develops in quite a different manner. Ralph Bingham…"

"I half promised to go and see a man——"

"But I will begin at the beginning," said the Sage. "I see that you are all impatience to hear the full details."

◦   ◦   ◦   ◦   ◦

Ralph Bingham and Arthur Jukes (said the Oldest Member) had never been friends—their rivalry was too keen to admit of that—but it was not till Amanda Trivett came to stay here that a smouldering distaste for each other burst out into the flames of actual enmity. It is ever so. One of the poets, whose name I cannot recall, has a passage, which I am unable at the moment to remember, in one of his works, which for the time being has slipped my mind, which hits off admirably this age-old situation. The gist of his remarks is that lovely woman rarely fails to start something. In the weeks that followed her arrival, being in the same room with the two men was like dropping in on a reunion of Capulets and Montagues.

You see, Ralph and Arthur were so exactly equal in their skill on the links that life for them had for some time past resolved itself into a silent, bitter struggle in which first one, then the other, gained some slight advantage. If Ralph won the May medal by a stroke, Arthur would be one ahead in the June competition, only to be nosed out again in July. It was a state of affairs which, had they been men of a more generous stamp, would have bred a mutual respect, esteem, and even love. But I am sorry to say that, apart from their golf, which was in a class of its own as far as this neighbourhood was concerned, Ralph Bingham and Arthur Jukes were a sorry pair—and yet, mark you, far from lacking in mere superficial good looks. They were handsome fellows, both of them, and well aware of the fact; and when Amanda Trivett came to stay they simply straightened their ties, twirled their moustaches, and expected her to do the rest.

But there they were disappointed. Perfectly friendly though

she was to both of them, the lovelight was conspicuously absent from her beautiful eyes. And it was not long before each had come independently to a solution of this mystery. It was plain to them that the whole trouble lay in the fact that each neutralized the other's attractions. Arthur felt that, if he could only have a clear field, all would be over except the sending out of the wedding invitations; and Ralph was of the opinion that, if he could just call on the girl one evening without finding the place all littered up with Arthur, his natural charms would swiftly bring home the bacon. And, indeed, it was true that they had no rivals except themselves. It happened at the moment that Woodhaven was very short of eligible bachelors. We marry young in this delightful spot, and all the likely men were already paired off. It seemed that, if Amanda Trivett intended to get married, she would have to select either Ralph Bingham or Arthur Jukes. A dreadful choice.

○　　○　　○　　○　　○

It had not occurred to me at the outset that my position in the affair would be anything closer than that of a detached and mildly interested spectator. Yet it was to me that Ralph came in his hour of need. When I returned home one evening, I found that my man had brought him in and laid him on the mat in my sitting-room.

I offered him a chair and a cigar, and he came to the point with commendable rapidity.

"Leigh," he said, directly he had lighted his cigar, "is too small for Arthur Jukes and myself."

"Ah, you have been talking it over and decided to move?" I said, delighted. "I think you are perfectly right. Leigh _is_ over-built. Men like you and Jukes need a lot of space. Where do you think of going?"

"I'm not going."

"But I thought you said——"

"What I meant was that the time has come when one of us must leave."

"Oh, only one of you?" It was something, of course, but I confess I was disappointed, and I think my disappointment must have shown in my voice; for he looked at me, surprised.

"Surely you wouldn't mind Jukes going?" he said.

"Why, certainly not. He really is going, is he?"

A look of saturnine determination came into Ralph's face.

"He is. He thinks he isn't, but he is."

I failed to understand him, and said so. He looked cautiously about the room, as if to reassure himself that he could not be overheard.

"I suppose you've noticed," he said, "the disgusting way that man Jukes has been hanging round Miss Trivett, boring her to death?"

"I have seen them together sometimes."

"I love Amanda Trivett!" said Ralph.

"Poor girl!" I sighed.

"I beg your pardon?"

"Poor girl!" I said. "I mean, to have Arthur Jukes hanging round her."

"That's just what I think," said Ralph Bingham. "And that's

why we're going to play this match."

"What match?"

"This match we've decided to play. I want you to act as one of the judges, to go along with Jukes and see that he doesn't play any of his tricks. You know what he is! And in a vital match like this——"

"How much are you playing for?"

"The whole world!"

"I beg your pardon?"

"The whole world. It amounts to that. The loser is to leave Leigh for good, and the winner stays on and marries Amanda Trivett. We have arranged all the details. Rupert Bailey will accompany me, acting as the other judge."

"And you want me to go round with Jukes?"

"Not round," said Ralph Bingham. "Along."

"What is the distinction?"

"We are not going to play a round. Only one hole."

"Sudden death, eh?"

"Not so very sudden. It's a longish hole. We start on the first tee here and hole out in the town in the doorway of the Majestic Hotel in Royal Square. A distance, I imagine, of about sixteen miles."

I was revolted. About that time a perfect epidemic of freak matches had broken out in the club, and I had strongly opposed them from the start. George Willis had begun it by playing a medal round with the pro., George's first nine against the pro.'s complete eighteen. After that came the contest between Herbert Widgeon and Montague Brown, the latter, a twenty-four handicap man, being entitled to shout "Boo!" three times during the round at moments selected by himself. There had been many more of these degrading travesties on the sacred game, and I had writhed to see them. Playing freak golf-matches is to my mind like ragging a great classical melody. But of the whole collection this one, considering the sentimental interest and the magnitude of the stakes, seemed to me the most terrible. My face, I imagine, betrayed my disgust, for Bingham attempted extenuation.

"It's the only way," he said. "You know how Jukes and I are on the links. We are as level as two men can be. This, of course is due to his extraordinary luck. Everybody knows that he is the world's champion fluker. I, on the other hand, invariably have the worst luck. The consequence is that in an ordinary round it is always a toss-up which of us wins. The test we propose will eliminate luck. After sixteen miles of give-and-take play, I am certain—that is to say, the better man is certain to be ahead. That is what I meant when I said that Arthur Jukes would shortly be leaving Leigh. Well, may I take it that you will consent to act as one of the judges?"

I considered. After all, the match was likely to be historic, and one always feels tempted to hand one's name down to posterity.

"Very well," I said.

"Excellent. You will have to keep a sharp eye on Jukes, I need scarcely remind you. You will, of course, carry a book of the rules in your pocket and refer to them when you wish to refresh your memory. We start at daybreak, for, if we put it off till later, the course at the other end might be somewhat congested when we reached it. We want to avoid publicity as far as possible. If I took a full iron and hit a policeman, it would excite a remark."

"It would. I can tell you the exact remark which it would excite."

"We will take bicycles with us, to minimize the fatigue of covering the distance. Well, I am glad that we have your co-operation. At daybreak tomorrow on the first tee, and don't forget to bring your rule-book."

○   ○   ○   ○   ○

The atmosphere brooding over the first tee when I reached it on the following morning, somewhat resembled that of a duelling-ground in the days when these affairs were sealed with rapiers or pistols. Rupert Bailey, an old friend of mine, was the only cheerful member of the party. I am never at my best in the early morning, and the two rivals glared at each other with silent sneers. I had never supposed till that moment that men ever really sneered at one another outside the movies, but these two were indisputably doing so. They were in the mood when men say "Pshaw!"

They tossed for the honour, and Arthur Jukes, having won, drove off with a fine ball that landed well down the course. Ralph Bingham, having teed up, turned to Rupert Bailey.

"Go down on to the fairway of the seventeenth," he said. "I want you to mark my ball."

Rupert stared.

"The seventeenth!"

"I am going to take that direction," said Ralph, pointing over the trees.

"But that will land your second or third shot in the lake."

"I have provided for that. I have a flat-bottomed boat moored close by the sixteenth green. I shall use a mashie-niblick and chip my ball aboard, row across to the other side, chip it ashore, and carry on. I propose to go across country as far as Woodfield. I think it will save me a stroke or two."

I gasped. I had never before realized the man's devilish cunning. His tactics gave him a flying start. Arthur, who had driven straight down the course, had as his objective the high road, which adjoins the waste ground beyond the first green. Once there, he would play the orthodox game by driving his ball along till he reached the bridge. While Arthur was winding along the high road, Ralph would have cut off practically two sides of a triangle. And it was hopeless for Arthur to imitate his enemy's tactics now. From where his ball lay he would have to cross a wide tract of marsh in order to reach the seventeenth fairway—an impossible feat. And, even if it had been feasible, he had no boat to take him across the water.

He uttered a violent protest. He was an unpleasant young man, almost—it seems absurd to say so, but almost as unpleasant as Ralph Bingham; yet at the moment I am bound to say I sympathized with him.

"What are you doing?" he demanded. "You can't play fast and loose with the rules like that."

"To what rule do you refer?" said Ralph, coldly.

"Well, that bally boat of yours is a hazard, isn't it? And you can't row a hazard about all over the place."

"Why not?"

The simple question seemed to take Arthur Jukes aback.

"Why not?" he repeated. "Why not? Well, you can't. That's why."

"There is nothing in the rules," said Ralph Bingham, "against moving a hazard. If a hazard can be moved without disturbing the ball, you are at liberty, I gather, to move it wherever you please. Besides, what is all this about moving hazards? I have a perfect right to go for a morning row, haven't I? If I were to ask my doctor, he would probably actually recommend it. I am going to row my boat across the sound. If it happens to have my ball on board, that is not my affair. I shall not disturb my ball, and I shall play it from where it lies. Am I right in saying that the rules enact that the ball shall be played from where it lies?"

We admitted that it was.

"Very well, then," said Ralph Bingham. "Don't let us waste any more time. We will wait for you at Woodfield."

He addressed his ball, and drove a beauty over the trees. It flashed out of sight in the direction of the seventeenth tee. Arthur and I made our way down the hill to play our second.

○   ○   ○   ○   ○

It is a curious trait of the human mind that, however little personal interest one may have in the result, it is impossible to prevent oneself taking sides in any event of a competitive nature. I had embarked on this affair in a purely neutral spirit, not caring which of the two won and only sorry that both could not lose. Yet, as the morning wore on, I found myself almost unconsciously becoming distinctly pro-Jukes. I did not like the man. I objected to his face, his manners, and the colour of his tie. Yet there was something in the dogged way in which he struggled against adversity which touched me and won my grudging support. Many men, I felt, having been so outmanoeuvred at the start, would have given up the contest in despair; but Arthur Jukes, for all his defects, had the soul of a true golfer. He declined to give up. In grim silence he hacked his ball through the rough till he reached the high road; and then, having played twenty-seven, set

himself resolutely to propel it on its long journey.

It was a lovely morning, and, as I bicycled along, keeping a fatherly eye on Arthur's activities, I realized for the first time in my life the full meaning of that exquisite phrase of Coleridge:

> _"Clothing the palpable and familiar
> With golden exhalations of the dawn,"_

for in the pellucid air everything seemed weirdly beautiful, even Arthur Juke's heather-mixture knickerbockers, of which hitherto I had never approved. The sun gleamed on their seat, as he bent to make his shots, in a cheerful and almost a poetic way. The birds were singing gaily in the hedgerows, and such was my uplifted state that I, too, burst into song, until Arthur petulantly desired me to refrain, on the plea that, though he yielded to no man in his enjoyment of farmyard imitations in their proper place, I put him off his stroke. And so we passed through Bayside in silence and started to cover that long stretch of road which ends in the railway bridge and the gentle descent into Woodfield.

Arthur was not doing badly. He was at least keeping them straight. And in the circumstances straightness was to be preferred to distance. Soon after leaving Little Hadley he had become ambitious and had used his brassey with disastrous results, slicing his fifty-third into the rough on the right of the road. It had taken him ten with the niblick to get back on to the car tracks, and this had taught him prudence.

He was now using his putter for every shot, and, except when he got trapped in the cross-lines at the top of the hill just before reaching Bayside, he had been in no serious difficulties. He was playing a nice easy game, getting the full face of the putter on to each shot.

At the top of the slope that drops down into Woodfield High Street he paused.

"I think I might try my brassey again here," he said. "I have a nice lie."

"Is it wise?" I said.

He looked down the hill.

"What I was thinking," he said, "was that with it I might wing that man Bingham. I see he is standing right out in the middle of the fairway."

I followed his gaze. It was perfectly true. Ralph Bingham was leaning on his bicycle in the roadway, smoking a cigarette. Even at this distance one could detect the man's disgustingly complacent expression. Rupert Bailey was sitting with his back against the door of the Woodfield Garage, looking rather used up. He was a man who liked to keep himself clean and tidy, and it was plain that the cross-country trip had done him no good. He seemed to be scraping mud off his face. I learned later that he had had the misfortune to fall into a ditch just beyond Bayside.

"No," said Arthur. "On second thoughts, the safe game is the one to play. I'll stick to the putter."

We dropped down the hill, and presently came up with the opposition. I had not been mistaken in thinking that Ralph Bingham looked complacent. The man was smirking.

"Playing three hundred and ninety-six," he said, as we drew near. "How are you?"

I consulted my score-card.

"We have played a snappy seven hundred and eleven." I said.

Ralph exulted openly. Rupert Bailey made no comment. He was too busy with the alluvial deposits on his person.

"Perhaps you would like to give up the match?" said Ralph to Arthur.

"Tchah!" said Arthur.

"Might just as well."

"Pah!" said Arthur.

"You can't win now."

"Pshaw!" said Arthur.

I am aware that Arthur's dialogue might have been brighter, but he had been through a trying time.

Rupert Bailey sidled up to me.

"I'm going home," he said.

"Nonsense!" I replied. "You are in an official capacity. You must stick to your post. Besides, what could be nicer than a pleasant morning ramble?"

"Pleasant morning ramble my number nine foot!" he replied, peevishly. "I want to get back to civilization and set an excavating party with pickaxes to work on me."

"You take too gloomy a view of the matter. You are a little

dusty. Nothing more."

"And it's not only the being buried alive that I mind. I cannot stick Ralph Bingham much longer."

"You have found him trying?"

"Trying! Why, after I had fallen into that ditch and was coming up for the third time, all the man did was simply to call to me to admire an infernal iron shot he had just made. No sympathy, mind you! Wrapped up in himself. Why don't you make your man give up the match? He can't win."

"I refuse to admit it. Much may happen between here and Royal Square."

I have seldom known a prophecy more swiftly fulfilled. At this moment the doors of the Woodfield Garage opened and a small car rolled out with a grimy young man in a sweater at the wheel. He brought the machine out into the road, and alighted and went back into the garage, where we heard him shouting unintelligibly to someone in the rear premises. The car remained puffing and panting against the kerb.

Engaged in conversation with Rupert Bailey, I was paying little attention to this evidence of an awakening world, when suddenly I heard a hoarse, triumphant cry from Arthur Jukes, and, turned, I perceived his ball dropping neatly into the car's interior. Arthur himself, brandishing a niblick, was dancing about in the fairway.

"Now what about your moving hazards?" he cried.

At this moment the man in the sweater returned, carrying a spanner. Arthur Jukes sprang towards him.

"I'll give you five pounds to drive me to Royal Square," he said.

I do not know what the sweater-clad young man's engagements for the morning had been originally, but nothing could have been more obliging than the ready way in which he consented to revise them at a moment's notice. I dare say you have noticed that the sturdy peasantry of our beloved land respond to an offer of five pounds as to a bugle-call.

"You're on," said the youth.

"Good!" said Arthur Jukes.

"You think you're darned clever," said Ralph Bingham.

"I know it," said Arthur.

"Well, then," said Ralph, "perhaps you will tell us how you propose to get the ball out of the car when you reach Royal Square?"

"Certainly," replied Arthur. "You will observe on the side of the vehicle a convenient handle which, when turned, opens the door. The door thus opened, I shall chip my ball out!"

"I see," said Ralph. "Yes, I never thought of that."

There was something in the way the man spoke that I did not like. His mildness seemed to me suspicious. He had the air of a man who has something up his sleeve. I was still musing on this when Arthur called to me impatiently to get in. I did so, and we drove off. Arthur was in great spirits. He had ascertained from the young man at the wheel that there was no chance of the opposition being able to hire another car at the garage. This machine was his own property, and the only other one at present in the shop was suffering from complicated trouble of the oiling-system and would not be able to be moved for at least another day.

I, however, shook my head when he pointed out the advantages of his position. I was still wondering about Ralph.

"I don't like it," I said.

"Don't like what?"

"Ralph Bingham's manner."

"Of course not," said Arthur. "Nobody does. There have been complaints on all sides."

"I mean, when you told him how you intended to get the ball out of the car."

"What was the matter with him?"

"He was too—ha!"

"How do you mean he was too—ha?"

"I have it!"

"What?"

"I see the trap he was laying for you. It has just dawned on me. No wonder he didn't object to your opening the door and chipping the ball out. By doing so you would forfeit the match."

"Nonsense! Why?"

"Because," I said, "it is against the rules to tamper with a hazard. If you had got into a sand-bunker, would you smooth away the sand? If you had put your shot under a tree, could your caddie hold up the branches to give you a clear shot? Obviously you would disqualify yourself if you touched that door."

Arthur's jaw dropped.

"What! Then how the deuce am I to get it out?"

"That," I said, gravely, "is a question between you and your Maker."

It was here that Arthur Jukes forfeited the sympathy which I had begun to feel for him. A crafty, sinister look came into his eyes.

"Listen!" he said. "It'll take them an hour to catch up with us. Suppose, during that time, that door happened to open accidentally, as it were, and close again? You wouldn't think it necessary to mention the fact, eh? You would be a good fellow and keep your mouth shut, yes? You might even see your way to go so far as to back me up in a statement to the effect that I hooked it out with my——?"

I was revolted.

"I am a golfer," I said, coldly, "and I obey the rules."

"Yes, but——"

"Those rules were drawn up by——"—I bared my head reverently—"by the Committee of the Royal and Ancient at St. Andrews. I have always respected them, and I shall not deviate on this occasion from the policy of a lifetime."

Arthur Jukes relapsed into a moody silence. He broke it once, crossing the West Street Bridge, to observe that he would like to know if I called myself a friend of his—a question which I was able to answer with a whole-hearted negative. After that he did not speak till the car drew up in front of the Majestic Hotel in Royal Square.

Early as the hour was, a certain bustle and animation already prevailed in that centre of the city, and the spectacle of a man in a golf-coat and plus-four knickerbockers hacking with a niblick at the floor of a car was not long in collecting a crowd of some dimensions. Three messenger-boys, four typists, and a gentleman in full evening-dress, who obviously possessed or was friendly with someone who possessed a large cellar, formed the nucleus of it; and they were joined about the time when Arthur addressed the ball in order to play his nine hundred and fifteenth by six news-boys, eleven charladies, and perhaps a dozen assorted loafers, all speculating with the liveliest interest as to which particular asylum had had the honour of sheltering Arthur before he had contrived to elude the vigilance of his custodians.

Arthur had prepared for some such contingency. He suspended his activities with the niblick, and drew from his pocket a large poster, which he proceeded to hang over the side of the car. It read:

COME
TO
McCLURG AND MACDONALD,
18, WEST STREET,
FOR
ALL GOLFING SUPPLIES.

His knowledge of psychology had not misled him. Directly they gathered that he was advertising something, the crowd declined to look at it; they melted away, and Arthur returned to his work in solitude.

He was taking a well-earned rest after playing his eleven hundred and fifth, a nice niblick shot with lots of wrist behind it, when out of Bridle Street there trickled a weary-looking golf-ball, followed in the order named by Ralph Bingham, resolute but going a trifle at the knees, and Rupert Bailey on a bicycle. The latter, on whose face and limbs the mud had dried, made an arresting spectacle.

"What are you playing?" I inquired.

"Eleven hundred," said Rupert. "We got into a casual dog."

"A casual dog?"

"Yes, just before the bridge. We were coming along nicely, when a stray dog grabbed our nine hundred and ninety-eighth and took it nearly back to Woodfield, and we had to start all over again. How are you getting on?"

"We have just played our eleven hundred and fifth. A nice even game." I looked at Ralph's ball, which was lying close to the kerb. "You are farther from the hole, I think. Your shot, Bingham."

Rupert Bailey suggested breakfast. He was a man who was altogether too fond of creature comforts. He had not the true golfing spirit.

"Breakfast!" I exclaimed.

"Breakfast," said Rupert, firmly. "If you don't know what it is, I can teach you in half a minute. You play it with a pot of coffee, a knife and fork, and about a hundred-weight of scrambled eggs. Try it. It's a pastime that grows on you."

I was surprised when Ralph Bingham supported the suggestion. He was so near holing out that I should have supposed that nothing would have kept him from finishing the match. But he agreed heartily.

"Breakfast," he said, "is an excellent idea. You go along in. I'll follow in a moment. I want to buy a paper."

We went into the hotel, and a few minutes later he joined us. Now that we were actually at the table, I confess that the idea of breakfast was by no means repugnant to me. The keen air and the exercise had given me an appetite, and it was some little time before I was able to assure the waiter definitely that he could cease bringing orders of scrambled eggs. The others having finished also, I suggested a move. I was anxious to get the match over and be free to go home.

We filed out of the hotel, Arthur Jukes leading. When I had passed through the swing-doors, I found him gazing perplexedly up and down the street.

"What is the matter?" I asked.

"It's gone!"

"What has gone?"

"The car!"

"Oh, the car?" said Ralph Bingham. "That's all right. Didn't I tell you about that? I bought it just now and engaged the driver as my chauffeur, I've been meaning to buy a car for a long time. A man ought to have a car."

"Where is it?" said Arthur, blankly. The man seemed dazed.

"I couldn't tell you to a mile or two," replied Ralph. "I told the man to drive to Glasgow. Why? Had you any message for him?"

"But my ball was inside it!"

"Now that," said Ralph, "is really unfortunate! Do you mean to tell me you hadn't managed to get it out yet? Yes, that is a little awkward for you. I'm afraid it means that you lose the match."

"Lose the match?"

"Certainly. The rules are perfectly definite on that point. A period of five minutes is allowed for each stroke. The player who fails to make his stroke within that time loses the hole. Unfortunate, but there it is!"

Arthur Jukes sank down on the path and buried his face in his hands. He had the appearance of a broken man. Once more, I am bound to say, I felt a certain pity for him. He had certainly struggled gamely, and it was hard to be beaten like this on the post.

"Playing eleven hundred and one," said Ralph Bingham, in his odiously self-satisfied voice, as he addressed his ball. He laughed jovially. A messenger-boy had paused close by and was watching the proceedings gravely. Ralph Bingham patted him on the head.

"Well, sonny," he said, "what club would _you_ use here?"

"I claim the match!" cried Arthur Jukes, springing up. Ralph Bingham regarded him coldly.

"I beg your pardon?"

"I claim the match!" repeated Arthur Jukes. "The rules say that a player who asks advice from any person other than his caddie shall lose the hole."

"This is absurd!" said Ralph, but I noticed that he had turned pale.

"I appeal to the judges."

"We sustain the appeal," I said, after a brief consultation with Rupert Bailey. "The rule is perfectly clear."

"But you had lost the match already by not playing within five minutes," said Ralph, vehemently.

"It was not my turn to play. You were farther from the pin."

"Well, play now. Go on! Let's see you make your shot."

"There is no necessity," said Arthur, frigidly. "Why should I play when you have already disqualified yourself?"

"I claim a draw!"

"I deny the claim."

"I appeal to the judges."

"Very well. We will leave it to the judges."

I consulted with Rupert Bailey. It seemed to me that Arthur Jukes was entitled to the verdict. Rupert, who, though an amiable and delightful companion, had always been one of Nature's fatheads, could not see it. We had to go back to our principals and announce that we had been unable to agree.

"This is ridiculous," said Ralph Bingham. "We ought to have had a third judge."

At this moment, who should come out of the hotel but Amanda Trivett! A veritable goddess from the machine.

"It seems to me," I said, "that you would both be well advised to leave the decision to Miss Trivett. You could have no better referee."

"I'm game," said Arthur Jukes.

"Suits _me_," said Ralph Bingham.

"Why, whatever are you all doing here with your golf-clubs?" asked the girl, wonderingly.

"These two gentlemen," I explained, "have been playing a match, and a point has arisen on which the judges do not find themselves in agreement. We need an unbiased outside opinion, and we should like to put it up to you. The facts are as follows:…"

Amanda Trivett listened attentively, but, when I had finished, she shook her head.

"I'm afraid I don't know enough about the game to be able to decide a question like that," she said.

"Then we must consult St. Andrews," said Rupert Bailey.

"I'll tell you who might know," said Amanda Trivett, after a moment's thought.

"Who is that?" I asked.

"My _fiancé_. He has just come back from a golfing holiday. That's why I'm in town this morning. I've been to meet him. He is very good at golf. He won a medal at Little-Mudbury-in-the-Wold the day before he left."

There was a tense silence. I had the delicacy not to look at Ralph or Arthur. Then the silence was broken by a sharp crack. Ralph Bingham had broken his mashie-niblick across his knee. From the direction where Arthur Jukes was standing there came a muffled gulp.

"Shall I ask him?" said Amanda Trivett.

"Don't bother," said Ralph Bingham.

"It doesn't matter," said Arthur Jukes.

ABOUT
THE AUTHOR

CARLO DE VITO is a publishing executive and sportswriter. He is the author of the *Ultimate Dictionary of Sports Quotations* and *Yogi: The Life and Times of an American Original.*

ABOUT CIDER MILL PRESS

Good ideas ripen with time. From seed to harvest, Cider Mill Press strives to bring fine reading, information, and entertainment together between the covers of its creatively crafted books. Our Cider Mill bears fruit twice a year, publishing a new crop of titles each spring and fall.

VISIT US ON THE WEB AT

www.cidermillpress.com

OR WRITE TO US AT

12 Port Farm Road
Kennebunkport, Maine 04046